*LEVITICUS 1-27:*
*For All People*

*Roman 6:23*

\* \* \*

*For the wages of sin is death;*
*but the gift of God is eternal life*
*through Jesus Christ our Lord.*

# LEVITICUS 1-27

## For All People

*'A Reminder Book - Remember'*

(Sin is serious, It comes with pay!)

## By: Maryland J. Harrison

"Child of the Most High and Only Living God"

ARPress
ILLUMINATING IDEAS
EMPOWERING VOICES

**ARPress**
45 Dan Road Suite 5
Canton MA 02021

Hotline:    1(888) 821-0229
Fax:         1(508) 545-7580

Ordering Information:

Quantity sales. Special discounts are available on quantity purchases by corporations, associations, and others. For details, contact the publisher at the address above.

Library of Congress Control Number:      2024904364
ISBN-13:         Softcover          979-8-89356-191-3
                 Hardcover          979-8-89356-190-6
                 eBook              979-8-89356-192-0

Printed and bound in The United States of America.

# CONTENTS

# INTRODUCTION

........................................

This is to remind the people of God our Heavenly Father, and the Lord Jesus Christ of all that was done for all people and to remember that they was brought with a price the blood of Jesus Christ our Lord and Savior. King of kings and Lord of lords. And that He is coming back again, the Bible is True. God want all to be saved. And there is a way that seems right to mankind but the end is destruction. Also, to remind the people that Heaven and Hell is Real, and that they should be working on their After Life, There is Life after Death from the Earth. Where they will spend Eternal Life. {Main Chapters for us today is 17 to 21 and more}.

*I am writing this reminder book in this way to help people focus on the Word of God, this is how the Lord brought the idea to me, so I wrote it down, to help the people, also myself. To remember God, and to remind you of His Word to us People. *I would start reading the Bible and, most always end of doing cross reference at times when I just wanted to read the Word of God. This is the book that I was lead or drawn to write first. *And I can see why just reading it again. The World some (People) are gone astray, we must keep Praying, for God's Mercy. Some People are sick and they don't even know they are. The evil spirits are in the World and in People at Large. I am a Born Again Christian, Child of the Most High God, Jehovah. And only Living God. Servant of the Lord Jesus Christ, God's only begotten Son. In whom I love.

*I am grateful to be alive and still here. I should be dead from drug, and other things. Car Accident, God protected, my husband and I. We were hit by a driver, speeding. I received a broken Pelvic Bone in six places. *I was penned inside the car passenger side, knocked out. I had to be cut out the car, my husband was in shock this was in 2005. And thank God we are still here in the world to try and encourage others when they are treated wrong, hurt and judged unfair, just trust God. Our Heavenly Father and He will help us.

*We are here to serve God, we have to go through to get through, Testimony. *I was drowning in SIN on my way to Hell. I was sick and tired of being sick and tired. I cried out to the Lord, to save me from my SIN, he heard and answered me. He delivered me from my SIN, SELF, SATAN and HELL FIRE, you see I believe in God, Heaven, and Satan is Real and He will be Casted into Hell the Lake of fire, this is real. *I am trying to remind the people, there is life after death. I believe in the Angels of God, and I know there are fallen angel, who are demons and devils now all Evil comes from Satan. I asked the Lord to SAVE me and He Came to Me, May 22, 1984.*

*I have been serving and living my life according to God's Holy Word the Bible, it is true you know. To the best of my ability The Holy Bible, Jesus Christ, God, Satan, the Devil. Angels and Demons. Are real. Believe it or not. God said choose Life. *I hope you are a believer. If not just pray right now, stop and ask the Father in Jesus Christ name to Forgive you of your SIN, and come into your Heart right now, and Lead and Guide you in the way He want you to go. Live and be a Witness for Him in this Earth. Look around you can see the destruction, if you are not a part of it. *Satan is a deceiver do the right things. Jesus is the same Yesterday, Today and Forever. He don't change! Hell is a real place. Will you be in Hell? Who will be in Hell? Don't let it be you. Hell is a place of punishment, for those that reject Jesus Christ, the Son of God, God's Gift to us, all people. *I wanted to write this book, also for those that don't believe that God is real and living, He is alive. Also, to try to give the people an easy way of reading the Word of God, it is so important to know what God said in His word for us, the way we are to live, not in SIN, that is Evil. I want to help you understand God's Word a little at a time. Very important to you, for your life, and Life after Death, we all will pass away. ***Where will you pass away to? Heaven or Hell, the Lake of**

**Fire. REPENT! Jesus Christ loves you more than you can ever think. Jesus is the Way, the Truth and the Life. Today and Forever.**

God meant what He said, and He said just what He meant in His Word to us, {Human beings.} His-Story to the people of the World. **{The Instructions - The Book, The Holy Bible}.** God started with Adam and later He made Eve, out of one of Adam's Ribs, think about that, and ask the Father to give you Wisdom, Knowledge and Understanding of His Word. God blessed us to be a blessing to others. To make this World a better place to live in. To worship Him (God), not ourselves, and other things. To follow Jesus Example! Also He said to pray for one another, and love one another, think what that could be if everybody in the whole wide World loved and prayed for each other, Heaven on Earth. *And helping others. No wars, No Greed, No Evil, No Hunger, No Pain. With God all thing are Possible.* **{True Pure Love -- Not Lust! No Homosexual, No Killing Innocent Babies.}**

*God our Heavenly Father loves every person, and He want us to follow the Word of Life, Jesus Christ the Living word came to Earth, to prepare the way for us to live. I love Him so, for sparing my life. Satan have been trying to destroy me before, I even knew who I was, and you also. He hates us. *God the Father, and Jesus Christ loves us all. I Love them too, do you? Do you really know who you are? Jesus gave His life for you! Have you given your life for Him. This Journey is all about God, His Son Jesus Christ and Accepting the Gift of Eternal Life and Living according to the Holy Bible. Not in Sin.

*If you want to know the Truth, Read the Holy Bible God's Word. You can start with this book Leviticus, for some understanding, my first Book. We must live according to the WORD. God made us to follow 'Jesus' example. That is if you want to go to Heaven when you pass away from Earth. The choice is yours, Heaven or Hell in the Lake of Fire. We need to know what God said and where we will spend our Eternal Life!

*Satan is trying to destroy you too, all that follow him, He hate you, He want to take you to Hell with him, if you don't **Repent and follow Jesus the Winner.**

**\* Satan is the Loser!** At the end of your life here on Earth you will live forever in Hell the Lake of Fire, if you don't turn from SIN. **\*SIN is not living according to the Word of God the Heavenly Father, the Truth. [And rejecting God's only Begotten Son Jesus Christ].**

*God the Father don't want us to go to the Lake of Fire, we are created in His Image we are Gods Children. I hope you are. *You know if you die without Christ in your heart, no amount of Money can save you from Hell Fire in the Lake.

**\*Please don't be deceived God is not mocked, whatever you sow, it will grow, and you will receive the fruits from your labor, Good, Bad or whatever you do. Right, Wrong. SIN is the reason. We are not animals, we are human beings. (We didn't come from animals, Darwin lied. We come from God, Human Being becoming like Jesus that is the Goal and Destiny for us. The People of God, all living in this World today, Stop and Think, this is Real).**

**\*Satan is the father of lies, he uses people, them that yield to him. I really need to warn you to turn from your SIN, if you are in SIN, the wages of SIN is Eternal Death, Separation from God the Father in Heaven. *And in your Heart!**

*And Hell is not going to be a Party, some people may say and thinking wrong. You can read in the Bible about Hell. What God say about it. *I am trying to help SAVE you for CHRIST sake, and yours. Jesus gave His life for us.

**\*Repent come back to God. I am a voice calling out to you Repent, follow the straight path. *Enter ye in at the strait gate: for wide is the gate, and broad is the way, that lead to destruction, and many there be which go in there, that lead to Eternal Death. Please don't let it be you, or anyone.**

*Heaven also you can read about it, you will be blessed. *For we know that if our earthly house of this tabernacle were dissolved, we have a building of God, a house not made with hands, Eternal in the Heavens. I am just trying to get the word out to those that don't believe the word of God. It is very true.

*We can't just live any kind of way we wish. Not good! Well, you can God give us a choice, but He want us to choose Life the right way, His way and Live forever with Him. {We love you!} {YOUR MONEY CAN'T SAVE YOU!}

*I had been bound on drugs, Alcohol and other things. I called out to the Lord God, and He heard me and answered He came to me, he delivered me. Now I need to tell everyone that will hear the words, read and receive. He will come to you also, if you ask Him. *Sin will take you some where you don't really want to go, deceive you.

*Jesus loves you more than you love yourself. Try Him! You might like Him, I know if you try Him you will fall in Love with Him, just like I have and so many other Brothers and Sisters. He died for us! Come on, Remember, you don't have to go to Hell. We Love You! Jesus Christ is the Way, the Truth and the Life. Accept His way and Live! [Read the Bible, Study it.]

*If you are reading this I pray that you will read all of the words, they will be a blessing to your Soul and Spirit I pray, and after you have read it go tell someone this is a blessing from the Lord God all Mighty our Heavenly Father. Believe, Unbelievers tell somebody. Read get Wisdom! Knowledge and Understanding of God's Word to You.

*I am just a Sister trying to tell Everybody, about Somebody, that can save Anybody. "JESUS SAVES!" This is real, If you are a believer now, I hope so, go tell someone, you are a Child of God now! Praise the Lord! Rejoice in Him! Get into Church, where the Word of God is being Taught, Lived, and Grow in the knowledge of God, and help others come to Christ.

*I want to draw the people back to reading the Bible again. What God the (Our) Heavenly Father told us in His word, and how we are to live our life, without sin, this is the Basic Instructions we need to follow Before Leaving Earth. {B-I-B-L-E}

*To miss Hell and Reach Heaven, our Heavenly Home. We are just passing through this land, we are on a Journey. {Pilgrims} {Are you passing the Test?} Don't be Deceived, Follow the Word of God the Holy Bible it is True, the Real Thing. Life in Christ. It is the only right way to live in this Life and the Life to come in Christ. There is Life after you die, and pass away from off the Earth. Don't die to find out the Bible is True after all. Trust and Believe God and His Word, Jesus Christ. **Amen!**

*Choose Life in Jesus Christ. Hear the word and be Doers of the Word of God Repent! Like John the Baptist, I am just a voice in the world calling all people, who hear to Repent come back to God the Heavenly Father. Save yourself from the Lake of Fire!

*Who told you that you can live anyway that you want to? Not God you know better than that, this is a wakeup Call, to Repent, turn from your Wicked ways and Pray and God will Heal the Land. And you also, just ask and receive in Jesus Christ Name. *You know your, Wrong! Are you?

**Examine yourself!**

**2 Chronicles 7:14 =** *If my people, which are called by my name, shall humble themselves, and pray, and seek my face, and turn from their wicked ways; then will I hear from heaven, and will forgive their sin, and will heal their land.

**Deuteronomy 8:18 =** *But thou shall remember the Lord thy God: for it is He that give thee power to get wealth, that he may establish his covenant which he swore unto thy fathers, as it is this day.

**Job 27:19-23 =** The rich man shall lie down, but he shall not be gathered: he opens his eyes, and he is not. Terrors take hold on him as waters, a tempest steal him away in the night. The east wind carries him away, and he departed: and as a storm hurled him out of his place. For God shall cast upon him, and not spare: he would fain flee out of his hand. Men shall clap their hands at him and shall hiss him out of his place.

**Matthew 10:28 =** And fear not them which kill the body, but are not able to kill the soul: but rather fear him which is able to destroy both soul and body in hell.

**Luke 16:23-31 =** And in hell, he lift up his eyes, being in torments, and sees Abraham afar off, and Lazarus in his bosom. *And he cried and said, Father Abraham, have mercy on me, and send Lazarus, that he may dip the tip of his finger in water, and cool my tongue; for I am tormented in this flame. *But Abraham said, Son, remember that thou in thy lifetime received thy good things, and likewise Lazarus evil things: but now he is comforted, and thou art tormented. *And beside all this, between us and you there is a great gulf fixed: so that they which would pass from hence to you cannot; neither can they pass to us, that would come from thence. *Then he said, I Pray thee therefore, father, that thou would send him to my father's house: *For I have five brethren; that he may testify unto them, lest they also come into this place of torment.

*Abraham said unto him, They have Moses and the prophets; let them hear them. *And he said, Nay, father Abraham: but if one went unto them from the dead, they will repent. *And he said unto him, If they hear not Moses and the prophets, neither will they be persuaded, though one rose from the dead.

**JESUS IS RISEN, HE DIED FOR OUR SINS, TOOK OUR PUNISHMENT ON HIM SELF. THE PEOPLE, THEY STILL DON'T BELIEVE. IF THEY DID, THIS WORLD WOULD BE A BETTER PLACE TO LIVE IN. JESUS CHRIST IS THE WAY, THE TRUTH AND THE LIFE. I WILL FOLLOW HIM.**

**JESUS CAME TO HEAL THE SICK, AND SET THE PEOPLE FREE. PEOPLE ARE SICK IN THE MIND. MAN WITH MAN, WOMAN WITH WOMAN, THAT IS PURE EVIL, SATAN WORSHIP. NOT GODS WILL! AND HAVING MORE THAN ONE WIFE TO ONE MAN, KILLING BABIE BEFORE THEY CAN EVEN LIVE. SAYING RIGHT IS WRONG & WRONG IS RIGHT, THAT IS SICKNESS FROM SATAN.**

**HE IS A DECEIVER, HE IS SO GOOD AT IT, HE WILL MAKE YOU BELIEVE A LIE. YOU MUST BE WISE AS A SERPENT AND GENTLE AS A DOVE. JUST A WARNING: BEFORE YOUR END, OUR END, THIS LIFE WILL COME TO AN END, AND WHERE WILL YOU SPEND YOUR ETERNAL LIFE?**

**THIS YOU NEED TO KNOW. SIN WILL TAKE YOU WHERE YOU DON'T WANT TO GO, MAKE YOU STAY**

**LONGER THAN YOU WANT TO STAY, AND MAKE YOU PAY MORE THAN YOU WANT TO PAY, AND YOU WILL PAY WITH YOUR LIFE, MONEY CAN'T SAVE YOU.**

I want to remind the Rich, Poor, Young, Old, Fat, Slim, Short, Tall, Little, Big, Skinny, all people who ever will, let them come to Jesus, wealthy Everybody. There is a way that Seems right to mankind, (People) but if we don't do right, the end is destruction.

*(In the Lake of Fire, with Satan the Devil his demons and the people that followed Satan and those that rejected Jesus Christ God's only Son). {That Loves You} {Turn around before it's too late!}*

Just a reminder in Love. Don't wait too late. God is calling YOU! Don't you hear Him calling your name? He loves you so Much. He gave His only Begotten Son for YOU and ME, answer the Call. **REPENT THIS THING IS REAL, DON'T BE LOST!**

This is no Joke and it sure is not funny, there is Life, Love, Joy, Peace, Happiness, Fruit and Laughter in Heaven, Everything we want Forever. I am going up yonder, to be with my Lord, I hope to see YOU there in the Name of Jesus Christ! Praying for YOU!

*The Body of Christ is Praying for you, the people everywhere always! Real Christians, what kind are you? You have to be Born Again. God knows who really Love Him. Do You?*

In Jesus Christ the SON of God the Father, Jehovah God, and the Holy Spirit, that is living inside of us, do you have Him, You need Him, We all need Him. More to come, if God is Pleased with this my **FIRST BOOK.** I have labored on. Thank God for the Word. HIS LOVE, MERCY AND GRACE FOR US, THE PEOPLE, HIS CREATION!

*This is the way I was led to write this Book. Remember the purpose is to get the People back to reading God's Holy Word.* I Pray the Lords will be done, thank you very much. For hearing my heart. Blessed is He or She that read the Word of God and Live by it, Be Doers of the Word of God. Not just hearers only.

**James 1:22-27**= But be ye doers of the word, and not hearers only, deceiving your own selves. *For if any be a hearer of the word, and not a doer, he is like unto a man beholding his natural face in a glass: *For he behold himself, and goes his way, and straightway forget what manner of man he was. *But whoso looked into the perfect law of liberty, and continued therein, he is being not a forgetful hearer, but a doer of the work, this man shall be blessed in his deed. *If any man among you seems to be religious, and bridled not his tongue, but deceived his own heart, this man's religion is vain. *Pure religion and undefiled before God and the Father is this, To visit the fatherless and widows in their affliction, and to keep himself unspotted from the world.

**Revelation 1:3-4=** Blessed is he that read, and they that hear the words of this prophecy, and keep those things which are written therein: for the time is at hand. *John said to the seven churches which are in Asia: Grace be unto you, and peace, from him which is, and which was, and which is to come; and from the seven Spirits which are before his throne.

**Revelation 14:13=** And I heard a voice from heaven saying unto me, Write, Blessed are the dead which die in the Lord from henceforth: Yes, said the Spirit, that they may rest from their labors; and their works do follow them.

In Jesus Name!

Praise the Lord God.

Love U! Your Sister, In Christ !

Maryland J. Harrison = Blessed & Chosen!

Child of the Most High and Only Living God.

In Jesus Christ Our Heavenly Father Abba.

And The Only Begotten Son of God!...

[A REMINDER BOOK THE BIBLE INSTRUCTIONS FOR LIFE]

"The way to Heaven, Holiness and wholeness"
To get closer to God our Father,
Basic Instructions Before Leaving Earth.

# LEVITICUS 1:1-17

........................................

## *The laws of Burnt offering*

And the Lord called unto Moses and spoke unto him out of the tabernacle of the congregation, saying, Speak unto the children of Israel, and say unto them.

***He {GOD} is speaking to you, and us all today)!***
***Listen and obey. Be blessed.***

If any man of you brings an offering unto the Lord, ye shall bring your offering of the cattle, even of the herd, and of the flock. If his offering be a burnt sacrifice of the herd, let him offer a male without blemish: he shall offer it of his own voluntary will at the door of the tabernacle of the congregation before the Lord.

***(The nations is robbing God, the nations of people***
***in tithes and offering Malachi 3:8-18).***

***Last book in the Old Testament read it and live, the TRUTH…***

And he shall put his hand upon the head of the burnt offering; and it shall be accepted for him to make atonement for him. And he shall kill the bullock before the Lord: and the priests, Aaron's sons, shall bring the blood, and sprinkle the blood round about upon the altar that is by the door of the tabernacle of the congregation. And he shall flay the burnt offering and cut it into his pieces. And the sons of Aaron the priest shall put fire upon the altar, and lay the wood in order upon the fire and the priests, Aaron's sons, shall lay the parts, the head, and the fat, in order upon the wood that is on the fire which is upon the altar: But his inwards and his legs shall he wash in water: and the priest shall burn all on the altar, to be a burnt sacrifice, an offering made by fire, of a sweet savour unto the Lord. And if his offering be of the flocks, namely, of the sheep, or of the goats, for a burnt sacrifice; he shall bring it a male without blemish.

And he shall kill it on the side of the altar northward before the Lord: and the priests, Aaron's sons, shall sprinkle his blood round about upon the altar. And he shall cut it into his pieces, with his head and his fat: and the priest shall lay them in order on the wood that is on the fire which is upon the altar: But he shall wash the inwards and the legs with water: and the priest shall bring it all and burn it upon the altar: it is a burnt sacrifice, an offering made by fire, of a sweet savour unto the Lord.

And if the burnt sacrifice for his offering to the Lord be of fowls, then he shall bring his offering of turtledoves, or of young pigeons. And the priest shall bring it unto the altar, and wring off his head, and burn it on the altar; and the blood thereof shall be wrung out at the side of the altar: And he shall pluck away his crop with his feathers, and cast it beside the altar on the east part, by the place of the ashes:

And he shall cleave it with the wings thereof but shall not divide it asunder: and the priest shall burn it upon the altar, upon the wood that is upon the fire: it is a burnt sacrifice, an offering made by fire, of a sweet savour unto the Lord.

# LEVITICUS 2:1-16

........................................

## *Meat offering*

A nd when any will offer a meat offering unto the Lord, his offering shall be of fine flour; and he shall pour oil upon it, and put frankincense thereon: And he shall bring it to Aaron's sons the priests: and he shall take there out his handful of the flour thereof, and of the oil thereof, with all the frankincense thereof; and the priest shall burn the memorial of it upon the altar, to be an offering made by fire, of a sweet savor unto the Lord: And the remnant of the meat offering shall be Aaron's and his sons': it is a thing most holy of the offerings of the Lord made by fire. And if thou bring an oblation of a meat offering bake in the oven, it shall be unleavened cakes of fine flour mingled with oil, or unleavened wafers anointed with oil.

And if thy oblation be a meat offering baked in a pan, it shall be of fine flour unleavened, mingled with oil. Thou shall part it in pieces and pour oil thereon: it is a meat offering. And if thy oblation be a meat offering baked in the frying pan, it shall be made of fine flour with oil.

And thou shall bring the meat offering that is made of these things unto the Lord: and when it is presented unto the priest, he shall bring it unto the altar. And the priest shall take from the meat offering a memorial thereof and shall burn it upon the altar: it is an offering made by fire, of a sweet savor unto the Lord. And that which is left of the meat offering shall be Aaron's and his sons': it is a thing most holy of the offerings of the Lord made by fire.

No meat offering, which ye shall bring unto the Lord, shall be made with leaven: for ye shall burn no leaven, nor any honey, in any offering of the Lord made by fire. As for the oblation of the first fruits, ye shall offer them unto the Lord: but they shall not be burnt on the altar for a sweet savor.

And every oblation of thy meat offering shall thou season with salt; neither shall thou suffer the salt of the covenant of thy God to be lacking from thy meat offering: with all thine offerings thou shall offer salt. And if thou offer a meat offering of thy first fruits unto the Lord, thou shall offer for the meat offering of thy first fruits green ears of corn dried by the fire, even corn beaten out of full ears.

And thou shall put oil upon it, and lay frankincense thereon: it is a meat offering. And the priest shall burn the memorial of it, part of the beaten corn thereof, and part of the oil thereof, with all the frankincense thereof: it is an offering made by fire unto the Lord.

# LEVITICUS 3:1-17

## Peace offering

And if his oblation be a sacrifice of peace offering, if he offers it of the herd; whether it be a male or female, he shall offer it without blemish before the Lord.

And he shall lay his hand upon the head of his offering and kill it at the door of the tabernacle of the congregation: and Aaron's sons the priests shall sprinkle the blood upon the altar round about. And he shall offer of the sacrifice of the peace offering an offering made by fire unto the Lord; the fat that covered the inwards, and all the fat that is upon the inwards.

And the two kidneys, and the fat that is on them, which is by the flanks, and the caul above the liver, with the kidneys, it shall he take away. And Aaron's sons shall burn it on the altar upon the burnt sacrifice, which is upon the wood that is on the fire: it is an offering made by fire, of a sweet savor unto the Lord. And if his offering for a sacrifice of peace offering unto the Lord be of the flock; male or female, he shall offer it without blemish. If he offers a lamb for his offering, then shall he offer it before the Lord.

And he shall lay his hand upon the head of his offering and kill it before the tabernacle of the congregation: and Aaron's sons shall sprinkle the blood thereof round about upon the altar. And he shall offer of the sacrifice of the peace offering an offering made by fire unto the Lord; the fat thereof, and the whole rump, it shall he take off hard by the backbone;

and the fat that covered the inwards, and all the fat that is upon the inwards. And the two kidneys, and the fat that is upon them, which is by the flanks, and the caul above the liver, with the kidneys, it shall he take away.

And the priest shall burn it upon the altar: it is the food of the offering made by fire unto the Lord. And if his offering be a goat, then he shall offer it before the Lord. And he shall lay his hand upon the head of it and kill it before the tabernacle of the congregation: and the sons of Aaron shall sprinkle the blood thereof upon the altar round about. And he shall offer thereof his offering, even an offering made by fire unto the Lord; the fat that covered the inwards, and all the fat that is upon the inwards.

And the two kidneys, and the fat that is upon them, which is by the flanks, and the caul above the liver, with the kidneys, it shall he take away. And the priest shall burn them upon the altar: it is the food of the offering made by fire for a sweet savor: all the fat is the Lord's. It shall be a perpetual statute for your generations throughout all your dwellings, that ye eat neither fat nor blood.

# LEVITICUS 4:1-35

........................................

## *Sin offering*

And the Lord spoke unto Moses, saying, Speak unto the children of Israel, saying, If a soul shall sin through ignorance against any of the commandments of the Lord concerning things which ought not to be done, and shall do against any of them:

If the priest that is anointed do sin according to the sin of the people; then let him bring for his sin, which he hath sinned, a young bullock without blemish unto the Lord for a sin offering. And he shall bring the bullock unto the door of the tabernacle of the congregation before the Lord; and shall lay his hand upon the bullock's head and kill the bullock before the Lord.

And the priest that is anointed shall take of the bullock's blood and bring it to the tabernacle of the congregation: And the priest shall dip his finger in the blood, and sprinkle of the blood seven times before the Lord, before the vail of the sanctuary. And the priest shall put some of the blood upon the horns of the altar of sweet incense before the Lord, which is in the tabernacle of the congregation; and shall pour all the blood of the bullock at the bottom of the altar of the burnt offering, which is at the door of the tabernacle of the congregation.

And he shall take off from it all the fat of the bullock for the sin offering; the fat that covered the inwards, and all the fat that is upon the inwards. And the two kidneys, and the fat that is upon them, which is by the flanks, and the caul above the liver, with the kidneys, it shall he take away. As it was taken off from the bullock of the sacrifice of peace offerings: and the priest shall burn them upon the altar of the burnt offering.

And the skin of the bullock, and all his flesh, with his head, and with his legs, and his inwards, and his dung. Even the whole bullock shall he carry forth without the camp unto a clean place, where the ashes are poured out, and burn him on the wood with fire: where the ashes are poured out shall he be burnt. And if the whole congregation of Israel sin through ignorance, and the thing he hid from the eyes of the assembly, and they have done somewhat against any of the commandments of the Lord concerning things which should not be done, and are guilty.

When the sin, which they have sinned against it, is known, then the congregation shall offer a young bullock for the sin and bring him before the tabernacle of the congregation. And the elders of the congregation shall lay their hands upon the head of the bullock before the Lord: and the bullock shall be killed before the Lord.

And the priest that is anointed shall bring of the bullock's blood to the tabernacle of the congregation: And the priest shall dip his finger in some of the blood, and sprinkle it seven times before the Lord, even before the vial.

And he shall put some of the blood upon the horns of the altar, which is before the Lord, that is in the tabernacle of the congregation, and shall pour out all the blood at the bottom of the altar of the burnt offering, which is at the door of the tabernacle of the congregation.

And he shall take all his fat from him and burn it upon the altar. And he shall do with the bullock as he did with the bullock for a sin offering, so shall he do with this: and the priest shall make an atonement for them, and it shall be forgiven them. And he shall carry forth the bullock without the camp and burn him as he burned the first bullock: it is a sin offering for the congregation.

When a ruler hath sinned, and done somewhat through ignorance against any of the commandments of the Lord his God concerning things which should not be done, and is guilty; Or if his sin, wherein he hath sinned, come to his knowledge; he shall bring his offering, a kid of the goats, a male without blemish:

And he shall lay his hand upon the head of the goat and kill it in the place where they kill the burnt offering before the Lord: it is a sin offering. And the priest shall take of the blood of the sin offering with his finger, and put it upon the horns of the altar of burnt offering, and shall pour out his blood at the bottom of the altar of burnt offering.

And he shall burn all his fat upon the altar, as the fat of the sacrifice of peace offerings: and the priest shall make an atonement for him as concerning his sin, and it shall be forgiven him. And if any one of the common people sin through ignorance, while he doeth somewhat against any of the commandments of the Lord concerning things which ought not to be done, and be guilty; Or if his sin, which he hath sinned, come to his knowledge: then he shall bring his offering, a kid of the goats, a female without blemish, for his sin which he hath sinned.

And he shall lay his hand upon the head of the sin offering and slay the sin offering in the place of the burnt offering. And the priest shall take of the blood thereof with his finger and put it upon the horns of the altar of burnt offering and shall pour out all the blood thereof at the bottom of the altar. And he shall take away all the fat thereof, as the fat is taken away from off the sacrifice of peace offerings; and the priest shall burn it upon the altar for a sweet savor unto the Lord; and the priest shall make an atonement for him, and it shall be forgiven him. And if he brings a lamb for a sin offering, he shall bring it a female without blemish.

And he shall lay his hand upon the head of the sin offering and slay it for a sin offering in the place where they kill the burnt offering. And the priest shall take of the blood of the sin offering with his finger, and put it upon the horns of the altar of burnt offering, and shall pour out all the blood thereof at the bottom of the altar:

And he shall take away all the fat thereof, as the fat of the lamb is taken away from the sacrifice of the peace offerings; and the priest shall burn them upon the altar, according to the offerings made by fire unto the Lord: and the priest shall make an atonement for his sin that he hath committed, and it shall be forgiven him.

# LEVITICUS 5:1-19

## *The Trespass offering*

And if a soul sin, and hear the voice of swearing, and is a witness, whether he hath seen or known of it; if he do not utter it, then he shall bear his iniquity. Or if a soul touches any unclean thing, whether it be a carcase of an unclean beast, or a carcase of unclean cattle, or the carcase of unclean creeping things, and if it be hidden from him; he also shall be unclean, and guilty.

Or if he touches the uncleanness of man, whatsoever uncleanness it be that a man shall be defiled withal, and it be hid from him; when he know of it, then he shall be guilty. Or if a soul swears, pronouncing with his lips to do evil, or to do good, whatsoever it be that a man shall pronounce with an oath, and it be hid from him; when he know of it, then he shall be guilty in one of these.

And it shall be, when he shall be guilty in one of these things, that he shall confess that he hath sinned in that thing: And he shall bring his trespass offering unto the Lord for his sin which he hath sinned, a female from the flock, a lamb or a kid of the goats, for a sin offering; and the priest shall make an atonement for him concerning his sin.

And if he be not able to bring a lamb, then he shall bring for his trespass, which he hath committed, two turtledoves, or two young pigeons, unto the Lord; one for a sin offering, and the other for a burnt offering. And he shall bring them unto the priest, who shall offer that which is for the sin offering first, and wring off his head from his neck, but shall not divide it asunder:

And he shall sprinkle of the blood of the sin offering upon the side of the altar; and the rest of the blood shall be wrung out at the bottom of the altar: it is a sin offering.

And he shall offer the second for a burnt offering, according to the manner: and the priest shall make an atonement for him for his sin which he hath sinned, and it shall be forgiven him. But if he be not able to bring two turtledoves, or two young pigeons, then he that sinned shall bring for his offering the tenth part of an Ephah of fine flour for a sin offering; he shall put no oil upon it, neither shall he put any frankincense thereon: for it is a sin offering.

Then shall he bring it to the priest, and the priest shall take his handful of it, even a memorial thereof, and burn it on the altar, according to the offerings made by fire unto the Lord: it is a sin offering. And the priest shall make an atonement for him as touching his sin that he hath sinned in one of these, and it shall be forgiven him: and the remnant shall be the priest's, as a meat offering.

And the Lord spoke unto Moses, saying, If a soul commits a trespass, and sin through ignorance, in the holy things of the Lord; then he shall bring for his trespass unto the Lord a ram without blemish out of the flocks, with thy estimation by shekels of silver, after the shekel of the sanctuary, for a trespass offering.

And he shall make amends for the harm that he hath done in the holy thing, and shall add the fifth part thereto, and give it unto the priest: and the priest shall make an atonement for him with the ram of the trespass offering, and it shall be forgiven him.

And if a soul sin, and commit any of these things which are forbidden to be done by the commandments of the Lord; though he wist it not, yet is he guilty, and shall bear his iniquity. And he shall bring a ram without blemish out of the flock, with thy estimation, for a trespass offering, unto the priest: and the priest shall make an atonement for him concerning his ignorance wherein he erred and wist it not, and it shall be forgiven him. It is a trespass offering: he hath certainly trespassed against the Lord.

# LEVITICUS 6:1-30

......................................

## *Trespass offering*

nd the Lord spoke unto Moses, saying, If a soul sin, and commit a
trespass against the Lord, and lie unto his neighbor in that, which
was delivered him to keep, or in fellowship, or in a thing taken away by
violence, or hath deceived his neighbor;

Or have found that which was lost, and lie concerning it, and swear
falsely; in any of all these that a man doeth, sinning therein: Then it shall
be, because he hath sinned, and is guilty, that he shall restore that which
he took violently away, or the thing which he hath deceitfully gotten, or
that which was delivered him to keep, or the lost thing which he found,

Or all that about which he hath sworn falsely; he shall even restore it
in the principal, and shall add the fifth part more thereto, and give it unto
him to whom it appertained, in the day of his trespass offering. And he
shall bring his trespass offering unto the Lord, a ram without blemish out
of the flock, with thy estimation, for a trespass offering, unto the priest:

And the priest shall make an atonement for him before the Lord:
and it shall be forgiven him for any thing of all that he hath done in
trespassing therein. And the Lord spoke unto Moses, saying, Command
Aaron and his sons, saying, This is the law of the burnt offering: It is the
burnt offering, because of the burning upon the altar all night unto the
morning, and the fire of the altar shall be burning in it.

And the priest shall put on his linen garment, and his linen breeches
shall he put upon his flesh and take up the ashes which the fire hath

consumed with the burnt offering on the altar, and he shall put them beside the altar. And he shall put off his garments, and put on other garments, and carry forth the ashes without the camp unto a clean place.

And the fire upon the altar shall be burning in it; it shall not be put out: and the priest shall burn wood on it every morning and lay the burnt offering in order upon it; and he shall burn thereon the fat of the peace offerings. The fire shall ever be burning upon the altar; it shall never go out. And this is the law of the meat offering: the sons of Aaron shall offer it before the Lord, before the altar.

And he shall take of it his handful, of the flour of the meat offering, and of the oil thereof, and all the frankincense, which is upon the meat offering, and shall burn it upon the altar for a sweet savor, even the memorial of it, unto the Lord. And the remainder thereof shall Aaron and his sons eat: with unleavened bread shall it be eaten in the holy place; in the court of the tabernacle of the congregation they shall eat it.

It shall not be baked with leaven. I have given it unto them for their portion of my offerings made by fire; it is most holy, as is the sin offering, and as the trespass offering. All the males among the children of Aaron shall eat of It. It shall be a statute forever in your generations concerning the offerings of the Lord made by fire: every one that touched them shall be holy.

And the Lord spoke unto Moses, saying, This is the offering of Aaron and of his sons, which they shall offer unto the Lord in the day when he is anointed; the tenth part of an ephah of fine flour for a meat offering perpetual, half of it in the morning, and half thereof at night. In a pan it shall be made with oil; and when it is baked, thou shall bring it in: and the baked pieces of the meat offering shall thou offer for a sweet savor unto the Lord. And the priest of his sons that is anointed in his stead shall offer it: it is a statute forever unto the Lord; it shall be wholly burnt. For every meat offering for the priest shall be wholly burnt it shall not be eaten.

And the Lord spoke unto Moses, saying, Speak unto Aaron and to his sons, saying, This is the law of the sin offering: In the place where the burnt offering is killed shall the sin offering be killed before the Lord:

it is most holy. The priest that offered it for sin shall eat it: in the holy place shall it be eaten, in the court of the tabernacle of the congregation. Whatsoever shall touch the flesh thereof shall be holy: and when there is sprinkled of the blood thereof upon any garment, thou shall wash that whereon it was sprinkled in the holy place.

But the earthen vessel wherein it is sodden shall be broken and if it be sodden in a brasen pot, it shall be both scoured, and rinsed in water. All the males among the priests shall eat thereof: it is most holy. And no sin offering, whereof any of the blood is brought into the tabernacle of the congregation to reconcile withal in the holy place, shall be eaten, it shall be burnt in the fire.

# LEVITICUS 7:1-38

........................................

## *The Guilt offering*

Likewise, this is the law of the trespass offering: it is most holy. In the place where they kill the burnt offering shall they kill the trespass offering: and the blood thereof shall he sprinkle round about upon the altar. And he shall offer of it all the fat thereof; the rump, and the fat that covered the inwards, And the two kidneys, and the fat that is on them, which is by the flanks, and the caul that is above the liver, with the kidneys, it shall he take away:

And the priest shall burn them upon the altar for an offering made by fire unto the Lord: it is a trespass offering. Every male among the priests shall eat thereof: it shall be eaten in the holy place: it is most holy. As the sin offering is, so is the trespass offering: there is one law for them: the priest that makes' atonement therewith shall have it. And the priest that offered any man's burnt offering, even the priest shall have to himself the skin of the burnt offering which he hath offered.

And all the meat offering that is baked in the oven, and all that is dressed in the frying pan, and in the pan, shall be the priest's that offered it. And every meat offering, mingled with oil, and dry, shall all the sons of Aaron have, one as much as another. And this is the law of the sacrifice of peace offerings, which he shall offer unto the Lord.

If he offers it for a thanksgiving, then he shall offer with the sacrifice of thanksgiving unleavened cakes mingled with oil, and unleavened wafers anointed with oil, and cakes mingled with oil, of fine flour, fried.

Besides the cakes, he shall offer for his offering leavened bread with the sacrifice of thanksgiving of his peace offerings.

And of it he shall offer one out of the whole oblation for a heave offering unto the Lord, and it shall be the priest's that sprinkled the blood of the peace offerings. And the flesh of the sacrifice of his peace offerings for thanksgiving shall be eaten the same day that it is offered; he shall not leave any of it until the morning. But if the sacrifice of his offering be a vow, or a voluntary offering, it shall be eaten the same day that he offered his sacrifice: and on the morrow also the remainder of it shall be eaten:

But the remainder of the flesh of the sacrifice on the third day shall be burnt with fire. And if any of the flesh of the sacrifice of his peace offerings be eaten at all on the third day, it shall not be accepted, neither shall it be imputed unto him that offered it: it shall be an abomination, and the soul that eat of it shall bear his iniquity.

And the flesh that touched any unclean thing shall not be eaten; it shall be burnt with fire: and as for the flesh, all that be clean shall eat thereof. But the soul that eat of the flesh of the sacrifice of peace offerings, that pertain unto the Lord, having his uncleanness upon him, even that soul shall be cut off from his people.

Moreover, the soul that shall touch any unclean thing, as the uncleanness of man, or any unclean beast, or any abominable unclean thing, and eat of the flesh of the sacrifice of peace offerings, which pertain unto the Lord, even that soul shall be cut off from his people. And the Lord spoke unto Moses, saying, Speak unto the children of Israel, saying. Ye shall eat no manner of fat, of ox, or of sheep, or of goat.

And the fat of the beast that die of itself, and the fat of that which is torn with beasts, may be used in any other use: but ye shall in no wise eat of it. For whosoever eat the fat of the beast, of which men offer an offering made by fire unto the Lord, even the soul that eat it shall be cut off from his people. Moreover, ye shall eat no manner of blood, whether it be of fowl or of beast, in any of your dwellings.

Whatsoever soul it be that eat any manner of blood, even that soul shall be cut off from his people. And the Lord spoke unto Moses, saying.

Speak unto the children of Israel, saying, He that offered the sacrifice of his peace offerings unto the Lord shall bring his oblation unto the Lord of the sacrifice of his peace offerings. His own hands shall bring the offerings of the Lord made by fire, the fat with the breast, it shall he bring, that the breast may be waved for a wave offering before the Lord.

And the priest shall burn the fat upon the altar: but the breast shall be Aaron's and his sons'. And the right shoulder shall ye give unto the priest for a heave offering of the sacrifices of your peace offerings. He among the sons of Aaron, that offered the blood of the peace offerings, and the fat, shall have the right shoulder for his part. For the wave breast and the heave shoulder have I taken of the children of Israel from off the sacrifices of their peace offerings and have given them unto Aaron the priest and unto his sons by a statute forever from among the children of Israel.

This is the portion of the anointing of Aaron, and of the anointing of his sons, out of the offerings of the Lord made by fire, in the day when he presented them to minister unto the Lord in the priest's office, Which the Lord commanded to be given them of the children of Israel, in the day that he anointed them, by a statute forever throughout their generations. This is the law of the burnt offering, of the meat offering, and of the sin offering, and of the trespass offering, and of the consecrations, and of the sacrifice of the peace offerings, Which the Lord commanded Moses in mount Sinai, in the day that he commanded the children of Israel to offer their oblations unto the Lord, in the wilderness of Sinai.

# LEVITICUS 8:1-36

························································

## *The Priests Portion*

And the Lord spoke unto Moses, saying, Take Aaron and his sons with him, and the garments, and the anointing oil, and a bullock for the sin offering, and two rams, and a basket of unleavened bread; And gather thou all the congregation together unto the door of the tabernacle of the congregation. And Moses did as the Lord commanded him; and the assembly was gathered together unto the door of the tabernacle of the congregation.

And Moses said unto the congregation, This is the thing which the Lord commanded to be done. And Moses brought Aaron and his sons and washed them with water. And he put upon him the coat, and girded him with the girdle, and clothed him with the robe, and put the ephod upon him, and he girded him with the curious girdle of the ephod and bound it unto him therewith.

And he put the breastplate upon him: also, he put in the breastplate the Urim and the Thummim. And he put the mitre upon his head; also, upon the mitre, even upon his forefront, did he put the golden plate, the holy crown; as the Lord commanded Moses. And Moses took the anointing oil, and anointed the tabernacle and all that was therein, and sanctified them. And he sprinkled thereof upon the altar seven times, and anointed the altar and all his vessels, both the laver and his foot, to sanctify them.

And he poured of the anointing oil upon Aaron's head, and anointed him, to sanctify him. And Moses brought Aaron's sons, and put coats upon them, and girded them with girdles, and put bonnets upon them, as the Lord commanded Moses.

And he brought the bullock for the sin offering: and Aaron and his sons laid their hands upon the head of the bullock for the sin offering. And he slew it; and Moses took the blood, and put it upon the horns of the altar roundabout with his finger, and purified the altar, and poured the blood at the bottom of the altar, and sanctified it, to make reconciliation upon it.

And he took all the fat that was upon the inwards, and the caul above the liver, and the two kidneys, and their fat, and Moses burned it upon the altar. But the bullock, and his hide, his flesh, and his dung, he burnt with fire without the camp, as the Lord commanded Moses. And he brought the ram for the burnt offering: and Aaron and his sons laid their hands upon the head of the ram.

And he killed it; and Moses sprinkled the blood upon the altar round about. And he cut the ram into pieces; and Moses burnt the head, and the pieces, and the fat. And he washed the inwards and the legs in water; and Moses burnt the whole ram upon the altar: it was a burnt sacrifice for a sweet savor, and an offering made by fire unto the Lord; as the Lord commanded Moses.

And he brought the other ram, the ram of consecration: and Aaron and his sons laid their hands upon the head of the ram. And he slew it; and Moses took of the blood of it and put it upon the tip of Aaron's right ear, and upon the thumb of his right hand, and upon the great toe of his right foot. And he brought Aaron's sons, and Moses put of the blood upon the tip of their right ear, and upon the thumbs of their right hands, and upon the great toes of their right feet: and Moses sprinkled the blood upon the altar round about.

And he took the fat, and the rump, and all the fat that was upon the inwards, and the caul above the liver, and the two kidneys, and their fat, and the right shoulder: And out of the basket of unleavened bread, that was before the Lord, he took one unleavened cake, and a cake of oiled bread, and one wafer, and put them on the fat, and upon the right shoulder: And he put all upon Aaron's hands, and upon his sons' hands, and waved them for a wave offering before the Lord.

And Moses took them from off their hands and burnt them on the altar upon the burnt offering: they were consecrations for a sweet savor: it is an offering made by fire unto the Lord. And Moses took the breast and waved it for a wave offering before the Lord: for of the ram of consecration it was Moses' part; as the Lord commanded Moses.

And Moses took of the anointing oil, and of the blood, which was upon the altar, and sprinkled it upon Aaron, and upon his garments, and upon his sons, and upon his sons' garments with him; and sanctified Aaron, and his garments, and his sons, and his sons' garments with him. And Moses said unto Aaron and to his sons, Boil the flesh at the door of the tabernacle of the congregation: and there eat it with the bread that is in the basket of consecrations, as I commanded, saying, Aaron and his sons shall eat it.

And that which remained of the flesh and of the bread shall ye burn with fire. And ye shall not go out of the door of the tabernacle of the congregation in seven days, until the days of your consecration be at an end: for seven days shall he consecrate you.

As he hath done this day, so the Lord hath commanded to do, to make an atonement for you. Therefore, shall ye abide at the door of the tabernacle of the congregation day and night seven days, and keep the charge of the Lord, that ye die not: for so I am commanded. So, Aaron and his sons did all things which the Lord commanded by the hand of Moses.

# LEVITICUS 9:1-24

........................................

## *Consecration of Priests*

And it came to pass on the eighth day, that Moses called Aaron and his sons, and the elders of Israel; And he said unto Aaron, Take thee a young calf for a sin offering, and a ram for a burnt offering, without blemish, and offer them before the Lord. And unto the children of Israel thou shall speak, saying, Take ye a kid of the goats for a sin offering; and a calf and a lamb, both of the first year, without blemish, for a burnt offering.

Also, a bullock and a ram for peace offerings, to sacrifice before the Lord; and a meat offering mingled with oil: for today the Lord will appear unto you. And they brought that which Moses commanded before the tabernacle of the congregation: and all the congregation drew near and stood before the Lord.

And Moses said, This is the thing which the Lord commanded that ye should do: and the glory of the Lord shall appear unto you. And Moses said unto Aaron, Go unto the altar, and offer thy sin offering, and thy burnt offering, and make an atonement for thyself, and for the people: and offer the offering of the people, and make an atonement for them; as the Lord commanded.

Aaron therefore went unto the altar, and slew the calf of the sin offering, which was for himself. And the sons of Aaron brought the blood unto him: and he dipped his finger in the blood, and put it upon the horns of the altar, and poured out the blood at the bottom of the altar: But the fat, and the kidneys, and the caul above the liver of the sin offering, he burnt upon the altar; as the Lord commanded Moses.

And the flesh and the hide he burnt with fire without the camp. And he slew the burnt offering; and Aaron's sons presented unto him the blood, which he sprinkled round about upon the altar. And they presented the burnt offering unto him, with the pieces thereof, and the head: and he burnt them upon the altar. And he did wash the inwards and the legs and burnt them upon the burnt offering on the altar.

And he brought the people's offering, and took the goat, which was the sin offering for the people, and slew it, and offered it for sin, as the first. And he brought the burnt offering and offered it according to the manner. And he brought the meat offering, and took a handful thereof, and burnt it upon the altar, beside the burnt sacrifice of the morning. He slew also the bullock and the ram for a sacrifice of peace offerings, which was for the people: and Aaron's sons presented unto him the blood, which he sprinkled upon the altar round about.

And the fat of the bullock and of the ram, the rump, and that which covered the inwards, and the kidneys, and the caul above the liver: And they put the fat upon the breasts, and he burnt the fat upon the altar: And the breasts and the right shoulder Aaron waved for a wave offering before the Lord; as Moses commanded. And Aaron lifted up his hand toward the people, and blessed them, and came down from offering of the sin offering, and the burnt offering, and peace offerings.

And Moses and Aaron went into the tabernacle of the congregation, and came out, and blessed the people: and the glory of the Lord appeared unto all the people. And there came a fire out from before the Lord and consumed upon the altar the burnt offering and the fat: which when all the people saw, they shouted, and fell on their faces.

# LEVITICUS 10:1-20

........................................

## *Priests Consecration*

And Nadab and Abihu, the sons of Aaron, took either of them his censer, and put fire therein, and put incense thereon, and offered strange fire before the Lord, which he commanded them not. And there went out fire from the Lord, and devoured them, and they died before the Lord.

Then Moses said unto Aaron, This is it that the Lord spoke, saying, I will be sanctified in them that come nigh me, and before all the people I will be glorified. And Aaron held his peace. And Moses called Mishael and Elzaphan, the sons of Uzziel the uncle of Aaron, and said unto them, Come near, carry your brethren from before the sanctuary out of the camp. So, they went near, and carried them in their coats out of the camp; as Moses had said.

And Moses said unto Aaron, and unto Eleazar and unto Ithamar, his sons, Uncover not your heads, neither rend your clothes; lest ye die, and lest wrath come upon all the people: but let your brethren, the whole house of Israel, bewail the burning which the Lord hath kindled. And ye shall not go out from the door of the tabernacle of the congregation, lest ye die: for the anointing oil of the Lord is upon you. And they did according to the word of Moses.

And the Lord spoke unto Aaron, saying, Do not drink wine nor strong drink, thou, nor thy sons with thee, when ye go into the tabernacle of the congregation, lest ye die: it shall be a statute forever throughout your generations: And that ye may put difference between holy and unholy, and between unclean and clean; And that ye may teach the children of Israel all the statutes which the Lord hath spoken unto them by the hand of Moses. And Moses spoke unto Aaron, and unto Eleazar and unto Ithamar, his sons that were left, Take the meat offering that remained of the offerings of the Lord made by fire, and eat it without leaven beside the altar: for it is most holy:

And ye shall eat it in the holy place, because it is thy due, and thy sons' due, of the sacrifices of the Lord made by fire: for so I am commanded. And the wave breast and heave shoulder shall ye eat in a clean place; thou, and thy sons, and thy daughters with thee: for they be thy due, and thy sons' due, which are given out of the sacrifices of peace offerings of the children of Israel.

The heave shoulder and the wave breast shall they bring with the offerings made by fire of the fat, to wave it for a wave offering before the Lord; and it shall be thine, and thy sons' with thee, by a statute forever as the Lord hath commanded. And Moses diligently sought the goat of the sin offering, and behold, it was burnt, and he was angry with Eleazar and Ithamar, the sons of Aaron which were left alive, saying,

Wherefore have ye not eaten the sin offering in the holy place, seeing it is most holy, and God hath given it you to bear the iniquity of the congregation, to make atonement for them before the Lord? Behold, the blood of it was not brought in within the holy place: ye should indeed have eaten it in the holy place, as I commanded.

And Aaron said unto Moses, Behold, this day have they offered their sin offering and their burnt offering before the Lord; and such things have befallen me: and if I had eaten the sin offering today, should it have been accepted in the sight of the Lord? And when Moses heard that, he was content.

# LEVITICUS 11:1-47

## *Clean and Unclean Animals*

And the Lord spoke unto Moses and to Aaron, saying unto them, Speak unto the children of Israel, saying, these are the beasts which ye shall eat among all the beasts that are on the earth. Whatsoever parted the hoof, and is cloven-footed, and chew the cud, among the beasts, that shall ye eat.

Nevertheless, these shall ye not eat of them that chew the cud, or of them that divide the hoof: as the camel, because he chew the cud, but divided not the hoof; he is unclean unto you.

And the Coney, because he cheweth the cud, but divided not the hoof; he is unclean unto you. And the hare, because he cheweth the cud, but divided not the hoof; he is unclean unto you. And the swine, though he divide the hoof, and be cloven-footed, yet he cheweth not the cud; he is unclean to you. Of their flesh shall ye not eat, and their carcase shall ye not touch; they are unclean to you.

These shall ye eat of all that are in the waters: whatsoever hath fins and scales in the waters, in the seas, and in the rivers, them shall ye eat. And all that have not fins, and scales in the seas, and in the rivers, of all that move in the waters, and of any living thing which is in the waters, they shall be an abomination unto you:

They shall be even an abomination unto you; ye shall not eat of their flesh, but ye shall have their carcasses in abomination. Whatsoever hath no fins nor scales in the waters, that shall be an abomination unto you. And these are they which ye shall have in abomination among the fowls; they shall not be eaten, they are an abomination: the eagle, and the ossifrage, and the ospray, And the vulture, and the kite after his kind; Every raven after his kind.

And the owl, and the night hawk, and the cuckow,
and the hawk after his kind,
And the little owl, and the cormorant, and the great owl,
And the swan, and the pelican, and the gier eagle,
And the stork, the heron after her kind,
and the lapwing, and the bat.
All fowls that creep, going upon all four,
shall be an abomination unto you.

Yet these may ye eat of every flying creeping thing that goes upon all four, which have legs above their feet, to leap withal upon the earth; Even these of them ye may eat; the locust after his kind, and the bald locust after his kind, and the beetle after his kind, and the grasshopper after his kind. But all other flying creeping things, which have four feet, shall be an abomination unto you.

And for these ye shall be unclean: whosoever touched the carcase of them shall be unclean until the even. And whosoever bear ought of the carcase of them shall wash his clothes and be unclean until the even. The car cases of every beast which divided the hoof, and is not cloven-footed, nor chew the cud, are unclean unto you: every one that touched them shall be unclean.

And whatsoever goes upon his paws, among all manner of beasts that go on all four, those are unclean unto you: whoso touched their carcase shall be unclean until the even. And he that bear the carcase of them shall wash his clothes and be unclean until the even: they are unclean unto you.

These also shall be unclean unto you among the creeping things that creep upon the earth; the weasel, and the mouse, and the tortoise after his kind, And the ferret, and the chameleon, and the lizard, and the snail, and the mole. These are unclean to you among all that creep: whosoever doth touch them, when they be dead, shall be unclean until the even.

And upon whatsoever any of them, when they are dead, doth fall, it shall be unclean; whether it be any vessel of wood, or raiment, or skin, or sack, whatsoever vessel it be, wherein any work is done, it must be put into water, and it shall be unclean until the even; so it shall be cleansed.

And every earthen vessel, where into any of them fall, whatsoever is in it shall be unclean; and ye shall break it. Of all meat which may be eaten, that on which such water cometh shall be unclean: and all drink that may be drunk in every such vessel shall be unclean. And everything whereupon any part of their carcase fall shall be unclean; whether it be oven, or ranges for pots, they shall be broken down: for they are unclean and shall be unclean unto you.

Nevertheless, a fountain or pit, wherein there is plenty of water, shall be clean: but that which touched their carcase shall be unclean. And if any part of their carcase falls upon any sowing seed which is to be sown, it shall be clean. But if any water be put upon the seed, and any part of their carcase fall thereon, it shall be unclean unto you.

And if any beast, of which ye may eat, die; he that touched the carcase thereof shall be unclean until the even. And he that eat of the carcase of it shall wash his clothes and be unclean until the even: he also that bear the car case of it shall wash his clothes and be unclean until the even.

And every creeping thing that creep upon the earth shall be an abomination; it shall not be eaten. Whatsoever go upon the belly, and whatsoever go upon all four, or whatsoever hath more feet among all creeping things that creep upon the earth, them ye shall not eat; for they are an abomination. Ye shall not make yourselves abominable with any creeping thing that creep, neither shall ye make yourselves unclean with them, that ye should be defiled thereby.

For I am the Lord your God: ye shall therefore sanctify yourselves, and ye shall be holy; for I am holy: neither shall ye defile yourselves with any manner of creeping thing that creep upon the earth. For I am the Lord that bring you up out of the land of Egypt, to be your God: ye shall therefore be holy, for I am holy.

This is the law of the beasts, and of the fowl, and of every living creature that move in the waters, and of every creature that creep upon the earth: To make a difference between the unclean and the clean, and between the beast that may be eaten and the beast that may not be eaten.

# LEVITICUS 12:1-8

## *Childbirth and Ceremonial Uncleanness*

And the Lord spoke unto Moses, saying, Speak unto the children of Israel, saying, If a woman has conceived seed, and born a man child: then she shall be unclean seven days; according to the days of the separation for her infirmity shall she be unclean. And in the eighth day the flesh of his foreskin shall be circumcised. And she shall then continue in the blood of her purifying three and thirty days; she shall touch no hallowed thing, nor come into the sanctuary, until the days of her purifying be fulfilled.

But if she bears a maid child, then she shall be unclean two weeks, as in her separation: and she shall continue in the blood of her purifying threescore and six days. And when the days of her purifying are fulfilled, for a son, or for a daughter, she shall bring a lamb of the first year for a burnt offering, and a young pigeon, or a turtledove, for a sin offering, unto the door of the tabernacle of the congregation, unto the priest:

Who shall offer it before the Lord, and make an atonement for her; and she shall be cleansed from the issue of her blood. This is the law for her that hath born a male or a female. And if she be not able to bring a lamb, then she shall bring two turtles, or two young pigeons; the one for the burnt offering, and the other for a sin offering: and the priest shall make an atonement for her, and she shall be clean.

# LEVITICUS 13:1-59

......................................

## *The Test of Leprosy*

A nd the Lord spoke unto Moses and Aaron, saying, When a man shall have in the skin of his flesh a rising, a scab, or bright spot, and it be in the skin of his flesh like the plague of leprosy; then he shall be brought unto Aaron the priest, or unto one of his sons the priests: And the priest shall look on the plague in the skin of the flesh: and when the hair in the plague is turned white, and the plague in sight be deeper than the skin of his flesh, it is a plague of leprosy: and the priest shall look on him, and pronounce him unclean. If the bright spot be white in the skin of his flesh, and in sight be not deeper than the skin, and the hair thereof be not turned white; then the priest shall shut up him that hath the plague seven days:

And the priest shall look on him the seventh day: and, behold, if the plague in his sight be at a stay, and the plague spread not in the skin; then the priest shall shut him up seven days more: And the priest shall look on him again the seventh day: and, behold, if the plague be somewhat dark, and the plague spread not in the skin, the priest shall pronounce him clean: it is but a scab: and he shall wash his clothes, and be clean.

But if the scab spread much abroad in the skin, after that he hath been seen of the priest for his cleansing, he shall be seen of the priest again. And if the priest sees that, behold, the scab spread in the skin, then the priest shall pronounce him unclean: it is a leprosy. When the plague of leprosy is in a man, then he shall be brought unto the priest.

And the priest shall see him: and, behold, if the rising be white in the skin, and it have turned the hair white, and there be quick raw flesh in the rising; It is an old leprosy in the skin of his flesh, and the priest shall pronounce him unclean, and shall not shut him up: for he is unclean. And if a leprosy breaks out abroad in the skin, and the leprosy cover all the skin of him that hath the plague from his head even to his foot, wheresoever the priest looked.

Then the priest shall consider: and, behold, if the leprosy have covered all his flesh, he shall pronounce him clean that hath the plague: it is all turned white: he is clean.

But when raw flesh appeared in him, he shall be unclean. And the priest shall see the raw flesh and pronounce him to be unclean: for the raw flesh is unclean: it is a leprosy. Or if the raw flesh turns again, and be changed unto white, he shall come unto the priest.

And the priest shall see him: and, behold, if the plague be turned into white; then the priest shall pronounce him clean that hath the plague: he is clean. The flesh also, in which, even in the skin thereof, was a boil, and is healed, And in the place of the boil there be a white rising, or a bright spot, white, and somewhat reddish, and it be showed to the priest;

And if, when the priest sees it, behold, it be in sight lower than the skin, and the hair thereof be turned white; the priest shall pronounce him unclean: it is a plague of leprosy broken out of the boil.

But if the priest looks on it, and, behold, there be no white hairs therein, and if it be not lower than the skin, but be somewhat dark; then the priest shall shut him up seven days: And if it spread much abroad in the skin, then the priest shall pronounce him unclean: it is a plague.

But if the bright spot stay in his place, and spread not, it is a burning boil; and the priest shall pronounce him clean. Or if there be any flesh, in the skin whereof there is a hot burning, and the quick flesh that burn have a white bright spot, somewhat reddish, or white; Then the priest shall look upon it: and, behold, if the hair in the bright spot be turned white, and it be in sight deeper than the skin; it is a leprosy broken out of the burning: wherefore the priest shall pronounce him unclean: it is the plague of leprosy.

But if the priest looks on it, and, behold, there be no white hair in the bright spot, and it be no lower than the other skin, but be somewhat dark; then the priest shall shut him up seven days: And the priest shall look upon him the seventh day: and if it be spread much abroad in the skin, then the priest shall pronounce him unclean: it is the plague of leprosy. *And if the bright spot stay in his place, and spread not in the skin, but it be somewhat dark; it is a rising of the burning, and the priest shall pronounce him clean: for it is an inflammation of the burning.*

If a man or woman have a plague upon the head or the beard; Then the priest shall see the plague: and, behold, if it be in sight deeper than the skin; and there be in it a yellow thin hair; then the priest shall pronounce him unclean: it is a dry scall, even a leprosy upon the head or beard. And if the priest looks on the plague of the scall, and, behold, it be not in sight deeper than the skin, and that there is no black hair in it; then the priest shall shut up him that hath the plague of the scall seven days:

And in the seventh day the priest shall look on the plague: and, behold, if the scall spread not, and there be in it no yellow hair, and the scall be not in sight deeper than the skin; He shall be shaven, but the scall shall he not shave; and the priest shall shut up him that hath the scall seven days more: And in the seventh day the priest shall look on the scall: and, behold, if the scall be not spread in the skin, nor be in sight deeper than the skin; then the priest shall pronounce him clean: and he shall wash his clothes, and be clean. But if the scall spread much in the skin after his cleansing; Then the priest shall look on him: and, behold, if the scall be spread in the skin, the priest shall not seek for yellow hair; he is unclean.

But if the scall be in his sight at a stay, and that there is black hair grown up therein; the scall is healed, he is clean: and the priest shall pronounce him clean. If a man also or a woman have in the skin of their flesh bright spots, even white bright spots;

Then the priest shall look: and, behold, if the bright spots in the skin of their flesh be darkish white; it is a freckled spot that growth in the skin; he is clean. And the man whose hair is fallen off his head, he is bald; yet is he clean. And he that hath his hair fallen off from the part of his head toward his face, he is forehead bald: yet is he clean.

And if there be in the bald head, or bald forehead, a white reddish sore; it is a leprosy sprung up in his bald head, or his bald forehead. Then the priest shall look upon it: and, behold, if the rising of the sore be white reddish in his bald head, or in his bald forehead, as the leprosy appeared in the skin of the flesh; He is a leprous man, he is unclean: the priest shall pronounce him utterly unclean; his plague is in his head.

And the leper in whom the plague is, his clothes shall be rent, and his head bare, and he shall put a covering upon his upper lip, and shall cry, Unclean, unclean. All the days wherein the plague shall be in him he shall be defiled; he is unclean: he shall dwell alone; without the camp shall his habitation be. The garment also that the plague of leprosy is in, whether it be a woollen garment, or a linen garment; Whether it be in the warp, or woof; of linen, or of woollen; whether in a skin, or in any thing made of skin;

And if the plague be greenish or reddish in the garment, or in the skin, either in the warp, or in the woof, or in any thing of skin; it is a plague of leprosy, and shall be showed unto the priest: And the priest shall look upon the plague, and shut up it that hath the plague seven days: And he shall look on the plague on the seventh day: if the plague be spread in the garment, either in the warp, or in the woof, or in a skin, or in any work that is made of skin; the plague is a fretting leprosy; it is unclean.

He shall therefore burn that garment, whether warp or woof, in woollen or in linen, or anything of skin, wherein the plague is: for it is a fretting leprosy; it shall be burnt in the fire. And if the priest shall look, and, behold, the plague be not spread in the garment, either in the warp, or in the woof, or in any thing of skin; Then the priest shall command that they wash the thing wherein the plague is, and he shall shut it up seven days more:

And the priest shall look on the plague, after that it is washed: and, behold, if the plague have not changed his color, and the plague be not spread; it is unclean; thou shall burn it in the fire; it is fret inward, whether it be bare within or without. And if the priest look, and, behold, the plague be somewhat dark after the washing of it; then he shall rend it out of the garment, or out of the skin, or out of the warp, or out of the woof:

And if it appear still in the garment, either in the warp, or in the woof, or in any thing of skin; it is a spreading plague: thou shall burn that wherein the plague is with fire.

And the garment, either warp, or woof, or whatsoever thing of skin it be, which thou shall wash, if the plague be departed from them, then it shall be washed the second time, and shall be clean. This is the law of the plague of leprosy in a garment of woollen or linen, either in the warp, or woof, or anything of skins, to pronounce it clean, or to pronounce it unclean.

# LEVITICUS 14:1-57

............................................

## *Cleansing of Lepers*

A nd the Lord spoke unto Moses, saying, This shall be the law of the leper in the day of his cleansing: He shall be brought unto the priest: And the priest shall go forth out of the camp; and the priest shall look, and, behold, if the plague of leprosy be healed in the leper;

Then shall the priest command to take for him that is to be cleansed two birds alive and clean, and cedar wood, and scarlet, and hyssop: And the priest shall command that one of the birds be killed in an earthen vessel over running water: As for the living bird, he shall take it, and the cedar wood, and the scarlet, and the hyssop, and shall dip them and the living bird in the blood of the bird that was killed over the running water:

And he shall sprinkle upon him that is to be cleansed from the leprosy seven times, and shall pronounce him clean, and shall let the living bird loose into the open field. And he that is to be cleansed shall wash his clothes, and shave off all his hair, and wash himself in water, that he may be clean: and after that he shall come into the camp and shall tarry abroad out of his tent seven days.

But it shall be on the seventh day, that he shall shave all his hair off his head and his beard and his eyebrows, even all his hair he shall shave off: and he shall wash his clothes, also he shall wash his flesh in water, and he shall be clean. And on the eighth day he shall take two he lambs without blemish, and one ewe lamb of the first year without blemish, and three tenth deals of fine flour for a meat offering, mingled with oil, and one log of oil.

And the priest that makes him clean shall present the man that is to be made clean, and those things, before the Lord, at the door of the tabernacle of the congregation. And the priest shall take one he lamb, and offer him for a trespass offering, and the log of oil, and wave them for a wave offering before the Lord: And he shall slay the lamb in the place where he shall kill the sin offering and the burnt offering, in the holy place: for as the sin offering is the priest's, so is the trespass offering: it is most holy:

And the priest shall take some of the blood of the trespass offering, and the priest shall put it upon the tip of the right ear of him that is to be cleansed, and upon the thumb of his right hand, and upon the great toe of his right foot: And the priest shall take some of the log of oil, and pour it into the palm of his own left hand:

And the priest shall dip his right finger in the oil that is in his left hand, and shall sprinkle of the oil with his finger seven times before the Lord: And of the rest of the oil that is in his hand shall the priest put upon the tip of the right ear of him that is to be cleansed, and upon the thumb of his right hand, and upon the great toe of his right foot, upon the blood of the trespass offering:

And the remnant of the oil that is in the priest's hand he shall pour upon the head of him that is to be cleansed: and the priest shall make an atonement for him before the Lord. And the priest shall offer the sin offering, and make an atonement for him that is to be cleansed from his uncleanness; and afterward he shall kill the burnt offering:

And the priest shall offer the burnt offering and the meat offering upon the altar: and the priest shall make an atonement for him, and he shall be clean. And if he be poor, and cannot get so much; then he shall take one lamb for a trespass offering to be waved, to make an atonement for him, and one tenth deal of fine flour mingled with oil for a meat offering, and a log of oil; And two turtledoves, or two young pigeons, such as he is able to get; and the one shall be a sin offering, and the other a burnt offering.

And he shall bring them on the eighth day for his cleansing unto the priest, unto the door of the tabernacle of the congregation, before the Lord. And the priest shall take the lamb of the trespass offering, and the log of oil, and the priest shall wave them for a wave offering before the Lord:

And he shall kill the lamb of the trespass offering, and the priest shall take some of the blood of the trespass offering, and put it upon the tip of the right ear of him that is to be cleansed, and upon the thumb of his right hand, and upon the great toe of his right foot: And the priest shall pour of the oil into the palm of his own left hand: And the priest shall sprinkle with his right finger some of the oil that is in his left hand seven times before the Lord:

And the priest shall put of the oil that is in his hand upon the tip of the right ear of him that is to be cleansed, and upon the thumb of his right hand, and upon the great toe of his right foot, upon the place of the blood of the trespass offering: And the rest of the oil that is in the priest's hand he shall put upon the head of him that is to be cleansed, to make an atonement for him before the Lord. And he shall offer the one of the turtledoves, or of the young pigeons, such as he can get;

Even such as he is able to get, the one for a sin offering, and the other for a burnt offering, with the meat offering: and the priest shall make an atonement for him that is to be cleansed before the Lord. This is the law of him in whom is the plague of leprosy, whose hand is not able to get that which pertained to his cleansing. And the Lord spoke unto Moses and unto Aaron, saying, When ye be come into the land of Canaan, which I give to you for a possession, and I put the plague of leprosy in a house of the land of your possession;

And he that owned the house shall come and tell the priest, saying, It seemed to me there is as it were a plague in the house: Then the priest shall command that they empty the house, before the priest go into it to see the plague, that all that is in the house be not made unclean: and afterward the priest shall go in to see the house: And he shall look on the plague, and, behold, if the plague be in the walls of the house with hollow strakes, greenish or reddish, which in sight are lower than the wall; Then the priest shall go out of the house to the door of the house, and shut up the house seven days:

And the priest shall come again the seventh day, and shall look: and, behold, if the plague be spread in the walls of the house; Then the priest shall command that they take away the stones in which the plague is, and they shall cast them into an unclean place without the city: And he shall cause the house to be scraped within round about, and they shall pour out the dust that they scrape off without the city into an unclean place:

And they shall take other stones and put them in the place of those stones; and he shall take other mortar and shall plaster the house. And if the plague come again, and break out in the house, after that he hath taken away the stones, and after he hath scraped the house, and after it is plastered; Then the priest shall come and look, and, behold, if the plague be spread in the house, it is a fretting leprosy in the house; it is unclean.

And he shall break down the house, the stones of it, and the timber thereof, and all the mortar of the house; and he shall carry them forth out of the city into an unclean place. Moreover, he that goeth into the house all the while that it is shut up shall be unclean until the even.

And he that lieth in the house shall wash his clothes; and he that eateth in the house shall wash his clothes. And if the priest shall come in, and look upon it, and, behold, the plague hath not spread in the house, after the house was plastered: then the priest shall pronounce the house clean, because the plague is healed.

And he shall take to cleanse the house two birds, and cedar wood, and scarlet, and hyssop: And he shall kill the one of the birds in an earthen vessel over running water: And he shall take the cedar wood, and the hyssop, and the scarlet, and the living bird, and dip them in the blood of the slain bird, and in the running water, and sprinkle the house seven times:

And he shall cleanse the house with the blood of the bird, and with the running water, and with the living bird, and with the cedar wood, and with the hyssop, and with the scarlet: But he shall let go the living bird out of the city into the open fields and make an atonement for the house: and it shall be clean.

This is the law for all manner of plague of leprosy, and scall, And for the leprosy of a garment, and of a house, And for a rising, and for a scab, and for a bright spot: To teach when it is unclean, and when it is clean: this is the law of leprosy.

# LEVITICUS 15:1-33

## The Uncleanness of Discharge

And the Lord spoke unto Moses and to Aaron, saying. Speak unto the children of Israel, and say unto them, When any man hath a running issue out of his flesh, because of his issue he is unclean. And this shall be his uncleanness in his issue: whether his flesh run with his issue, or his flesh be stopped from his issue, it is his uncleanness.

Every bed, whereon he lieth that hath the issue, is unclean: and everything, whereon he sitteth, shall be unclean. And whosoever touched his bed shall wash his clothes, and bathe himself in water, and be unclean until the even. And he that sitteth on anything whereon he sat that hath the issue shall wash his clothes, and bathe himself in water, and be unclean until the even.

And he that touched the flesh of him that hath the issue shall wash his clothes, and bathe himself in water, and be unclean until the even. And if he that hath the issue spit upon him that is clean; then he shall wash his clothes, and bathe himself in water, and be unclean until the even. And what saddle so ever he rides upon that hath the issue shall be unclean.

And whosoever touched anything that was under him shall be unclean until the even: and he that beareth any of those things shall wash his clothes, and bathe himself in water, and be unclean until the even.

And whomsoever he touched that hath the issue, and hath not rinsed his hands in water, he shall wash his clothes, and bathe himself in water, and be unclean until the even. And the vessel of earth, that he touched which hath the issue, shall be broken: and every vessel of wood shall be rinsed in water. And when he that hath an issue is cleansed of his issue; then he shall number to himself seven days for his cleansing, and wash his clothes, and bathe his flesh in running water, and shall be clean.

And on the eighth day he shall take to him two turtledoves, or two young pigeons, and come before the Lord unto the door of the tabernacle of the congregation, and give them unto the Priest.

And the priest shall offer them, the one for a sin offering, and the other for a burnt offering; and the priest shall make an atonement for him before the Lord for his issue. And if any man's seed of copulation go out from him, then he shall wash all his flesh in water, and be unclean until the even. And every garment, and every skin, whereon is the seed of copulation, shall be washed with water, and be unclean until the even. The woman also with whom man shall lie with seed of copulation, they shall both bathe themselves in water, and be unclean until the even.

And if a woman has an issue, and her issue in her flesh be blood, she shall be put apart seven days: and whosoever touched her shall be unclean until the even. And everything that she lieth upon in her separation shall be unclean: everything also that she sits upon shall be unclean. And whosoever touched her bed shall wash his clothes, and bathe himself in water, and be unclean until the even. And whosoever touched anything that she sat upon shall wash his clothes, and bathe himself in water, and be unclean until the even.

And if it be on her bed, or on anything whereon she sits, when he touched it, he shall be unclean until the even. And if any man lies with her at all, and her flowers be upon him, he shall be unclean seven days; and all the bed whereon he lieth shall be unclean. And if a woman has an issue of her blood many days out of the time of her separation, or if it run beyond the time of her separation; all the days of the issue of her uncleanness shall be as the days of her separation: she shall be unclean.

Every bed whereon she lieth all the days of her issue shall be unto her as the bed of her separation: and whatsoever she sitteth upon shall be unclean, as the uncleanness of her separation. And whosoever touched those things shall be unclean, and shall wash his clothes, and bathe himself in water, and be unclean until the even.

But if she be cleansed of her issue, then she shall number to herself seven days, and after that she shall be clean. And on the eighth day she shall take unto her two turtles, or two young pigeons, and bring them unto the priest, to the door of the tabernacle of the congregation. And the priest shall offer the one for a sin offering, and the other for a burnt offering; and the priest shall make an atonement for her before the Lord for the issue of her uncleanness.

Thus, shall ye separate the children of Israel from their uncleanness; that they die not in their uncleanness, when they defile my tabernacle that is among them. This is the law of him that hath an issue, and of him whose seed goeth from him, and is defiled there with; And of her that is sick of her flowers, and of him that hath an issue, of the man, and of the woman, and of him that lieth with her that is unclean.

# LEVITICUS 16:1-34

......................................

## *The Ritual of Atonement*

And the Lord spoke unto Moses after the death of the two sons of Aaron, when they offered before the Lord, and died; And the Lord said unto Moses, Speak unto Aaron thy brother, that he come not at all times into the holy place within the vail before the mercy seat, which is upon the ark; that he die not: for I will appear in the cloud upon the mercy seat. Thus, shall Aaron come into the holy place: with a young bullock for a sin offering, and a ram for a burnt offering.

He shall put on the holy linen coat, and he shall have the linen breeches upon his flesh, and shall be girded with a linen girdle, and with the linen mitre shall he be attired: these are holy garments; therefore shall he wash his flesh in water, and so put them on.

And he shall take of the congregation of the children of Israel two kids of the goats for a sin offering, and one ram for a burnt offering.

And Aaron shall offer his bullock of the sin offering, which is for himself, and make an atonement for himself, and for his house. And he shall take the two goats and present them before the Lord at the door of the tabernacle of the congregation. And Aaron shall cast lots upon the two goats; one lot for the Lord, and the other lot for the scapegoat. And Aaron shall bring the goat upon which the Lord's lot fell and offer him for a sin offering. But the goat, on which the lot fell to be the scapegoat, shall be presented alive before the Lord, to make an atonement with him, and to let him go for a scapegoat into the wilderness.

And Aaron shall bring the bullock of the sin offering, which is for himself, and shall make an atonement for himself, and for his house, and shall kill the bullock of the sin offering which is for himself: And he shall take a censer full of burning coals of fire from off the altar before the Lord, and his hands full of sweet incense beaten small, and bring it within the vail:

And he shall put the incense upon the fire before the Lord, that the cloud of the incense may cover the mercy seat that is upon the testimony, that he die not: And he shall take of the blood of the bullock, and sprinkle it with his finger upon the mercy seat eastward; and before the mercy seat shall he sprinkle of the blood with his finger seven times.

Then shall he kill the goat of the sin offering, that is for the people, and bring his blood within the vail, and do with that blood as he did with the blood of the bullock, and sprinkle it upon the mercy seat, and before the mercy seat: And he shall make an atonement for the holy place, because of the uncleanness of the children of Israel, and because of their transgressions in all their sins: and so shall he do for the tabernacle of the congregation, that remaineth among them in the midst of their uncleanness.

And there shall be no man in the tabernacle of the congregation when he goeth in to make an atonement in the holy place, until he come out, and have made an atonement for himself, and for his household, and for all the congregation of Israel. And he shall go out unto the altar that is before the Lord and make an atonement for it; and shall take of the blood of the bullock, and of the blood of the goat, and put it upon the horns of the altar round about.

And he shall sprinkle of the blood upon it with his finger seven times, and cleanse it, and hallow it from the uncleanness of the children of Israel. And when he hath made an end of reconciling the holy place, and the tabernacle of the congregation, and the altar, he shall bring the live goat: And Aaron shall lay both his hands upon the head of the live goat, and confess over him all the iniquities of the children of Israel, and all their transgressions in all their sins, putting them upon the head of the goat, and shall send him away by the hand of a fit man into the wilderness:

And the goat shall bear upon him all their iniquities unto a land not inhabited: and he shall let go the goat in the wilderness. And Aaron shall come into the tabernacle of the congregation, and shall put off the linen garments, which he put on when he went into the holy place and shall leave them there: And he shall wash his flesh with water in the holy place, and put on his garments, and come forth, and offer his burnt offering, and the burnt offering of the people, and make an atonement for himself, and for the people.

And the fat of the sin offering shall he burn upon the altar. And he that let go the goat for the scapegoat shall wash his clothes, and bathe his flesh in water, and afterward come into the camp. And the bullock for the sin offering, and the goat for the sin offering, whose blood was brought in to make atonement in the holy place, shall one carry forth without the camp; and they shall burn in the fire their skins, and their flesh, and their dung. And he that burned them shall wash his clothes, and bathe his flesh in water, and afterward he shall come into the camp.

And this shall be a statute forever unto you: that in the seventh month, on the tenth day of the month, ye shall afflict your souls, and do no work at all, whether it be one of your own country, or a stranger that sojourned among you: For on that day shall the priest make an atonement for you, to cleanse you, that ye may be clean from all your sins before the Lord. It shall be a Sabbath of rest unto you, and ye shall afflict your souls, by a statute forever.

And the priest, whom he shall anoint, and whom he shall consecrate to minister in the priest's office in his father's stead, shall make the atonement, and shall put on the linen clothes, even the holy garments: And he shall make an atonement for the holy sanctuary, and he shall make an atonement for the tabernacle of the congregation, and for the altar, and he shall make an atonement for the priests, and for all the people of the congregation.

And this shall be an everlasting statute unto you, to make an atonement for the children of Israel for all their sins once a year. And he did as the Lord commanded Moses.

# LEVITICUS 17:1-16

## *Eating of Blood Forbidden*

And the Lord spoke unto Moses, saying, Speak unto Aaron, and unto his sons, and unto all the children of Israel, and say unto them; This is the thing which the Lord hath commanded, saying, What man so ever there be of the house of Israel, that killed an ox, or lamb, or goat, in the camp, or that killed it out of the camp,

And bring it not unto the door of the tabernacle of the congregation, to offer an offering unto the Lord before the tabernacle of the Lord; blood shall be imputed unto that man; he hath shed blood; and that man shall be cut off from among his people:

To the end that the children of Israel may bring their sacrifices, which they offer in the open field, even that they may bring them unto the Lord, unto the door of the tabernacle of the congregation, unto the priest, and offer them for peace offerings unto the Lord. And the priest shall sprinkle the blood upon the altar of the Lord at the door of the tabernacle of the congregation and burn the fat for a sweet savor unto the Lord.

### *(And they shall no more offers their sacrifices unto devils, after whom they have gone a whoring).*

This shall be a statute forever unto them throughout their generations. And thou shall say unto them, Whatsoever man there be of the house of Israel, or of the strangers which sojourn among you, that offered a burnt offering or sacrifice, And bring it not unto the door of the tabernacle of the congregation, to offer it unto the Lord; even that man shall be cut off from among his people.

And whatsoever man there be of the house of Israel, or of the strangers that sojourn among you, that eat any manner of blood; I will even set my face against that soul that eat blood and will cut him off from among his people. For the life of the flesh is in the blood: and I have given it to you upon the altar to make an atonement for your souls: for it is the blood that makes an atonement for the soul. Therefore, I said unto the children of Israel.

No soul of you shall eat blood, neither shall any stranger that sojourned among you eat blood. *And whatsoever man there be of the children of Israel, or of the strangers that sojourn* among you, which hunted and catches any beast or fowl that may be eaten; he shall even pour out the blood thereof and cover it with dust.

For it is the life of all flesh; the blood of it is for the life thereof: therefore, I said unto the children of Israel. Ye shall eat the blood of **no** manner of flesh: for the life of all flesh is the blood thereof: whosoever eat it shall be cut off. And every soul that eat that which died of itself, or that which was torn with beasts, whether it be one of your own country, or a stranger, he shall both wash his clothes, and bathe himself in water, and be unclean until the even: then shall he be clean. <u>But if he wash them not, nor bathe his flesh; then he shall bear his iniquity</u>. **(SIN)**

### 'Unlawful marriages and lust'

*<u>To live a pure, wholesome, and Holy life.</u>*
*<u>"Disease free, Sin is the Reason."</u>*

# LEVITICUS 18:1-30

......................................

## *'Laws of Righteousness'*

And the Lord spoke unto Moses, saying, Speak unto the children of Israel, and say unto them, I am the Lord your God. After the doings of the land of Egypt, wherein ye dwelt, shall ye not do: and after the doings of the land of Canaan, whither I bring you, shall ye not do: neither shall ye walk in their ordinances.

### (Nakedness-Mean to have Sexual Relation!)

Ye shall do my judgments, and keep mine ordinances, to walk therein: I am the Lord your God. Ye shall therefore keep my statutes, and my judgments: which if a man do, he shall live in them: I am the Lord.

None of you shall approach to any that is near of kin to him, to uncover their nakedness: I am the Lord. (Sexually)

*The nakedness of thy father, or the nakedness of thy mother, shall thou not uncover: she is thy mother; thou shall not uncover her nakedness.

*The nakedness of thy father's wife shall thou not uncover: it is thy father's nakedness.

*The nakedness of thy sister, the daughter of thy father, or daughter of thy mother, whether she be born at home, or born abroad, even their nakedness thou shall not uncover.

*The nakedness of thy son's daughter, or of thy daughter's daughter, even their nakedness thou shall not uncover: for theirs is thine own nakedness.

*The nakedness of thy father's wife's daughter, begotten of thy father, she is thy sister, thou shall not uncover her nakedness.

*Thou shall not uncover the nakedness of thy father's sister: she is thy father's near kinswoman.

*Thou shall not uncover the nakedness of thy mother's sister: for she is thy mother's near kinswoman.

*Thou shall not uncover the nakedness of thy father's brother, thou shall not approach to his wife: she is thine aunt.

*Thou shall not uncover the nakedness of thy daughter in law: she is thy son's wife; thou shall not uncover her nakedness.

*Thou shall not uncover the nakedness of thy brother's wife: it is thy brother's nakedness.

*Thou shall not uncover the nakedness of a woman and her daughter, neither shall thou take her son's daughter, or her daughter's daughter, to uncover her nakedness; for they are her near kinswomen: it is wickedness.

*Neither shall thou take a wife to her sister, to vex her, to uncover her nakedness, beside the other in her lifetime.

*Also, thou shall not approach unto a woman to uncover her nakedness, as long as she is put apart for her uncleanness.

*Moreover, thou shall not lie carnally with thy neighbor's wife, to defile thyself with her. *And thou shall not let any of thy seed pass through the fire to Molech, neither shall thou profane the name of thy God: I am the Lord. *_Thou shall not lie with mankind, as with womankind: it is abomination. *Neither shall thou lie with any beast to_ *defile thyself therewith: neither shall any woman stand before a beast to lie down thereto: it is confusion.*

(SIN-SICK-MIND) JESUS CAME TO HEAL THE SICK. REPENT! BE HEALED, IN THE NAME OF JESUS CHRIST. BY HIS STRIPE WE WERE HEALED. BY HIS BLOOD, HE SHED FOR US, AND HE IS ALIVE TODAY!

*Defile not ye yourselves in any of these things: for in all these the nations are defiled which I cast out before you:

*And the land is defiled: therefore, I do visit the iniquity thereof upon it, and the land itself vomited out her inhabitants.

*Ye shall therefore keep my statutes and my judgments, and shall not commit any of these abominations; neither any of your own nation, nor any stranger that sojourned among you:

*(For all these abominations have the men of the land done, which were before you, and the land is defiled;) That the land spue not you out also, when ye defile it, as it spued out the nations that were before you.

*For whosoever shall commit any of these abominations, even the souls that commit them shall be cut off from among their people.

*Therefore, shall ye keep mine ordinance, that ye commit not any one of these abominable customs, which were committed before you, and that ye defile not yourselves therein: I am the Lord your God.

# LEVITICUS 19:1-37

## Laws of Righteousness-Holy Living

nd the Lord spoke unto Moses, saying, Speak unto all the congregation of the children of Israel, and say unto them, Ye shall be holy: for I the Lord your God am holy. Ye shall fear every man his mother, and his father, and keep my Sabbaths:

I am the Lord your God. Turn ye not unto idols, nor make to yourselves molten gods: I am the Lord your God.

And if ye offer a sacrifice of peace offerings unto the Lord, ye shall offer it at your own will. It shall be eaten the same day ye offer it, and on the morrow: and if ought to remain until the third day, it shall be burnt in the fire.

And if it be eaten at all on the third day, it is abominable; it shall not be accepted. Therefore, everyone that eateth it shall bear his iniquity, because he hath profaned the hallowed thing of the Lord: and that soul shall be cut off from among his people.

And when ye reap the harvest of your land, thou shall not wholly reap the corners of thy field, neither shall thou gather the gleanings of thy harvest. And thou shall not glean thy vineyard, neither shall thou gather every grape of thy vineyard; thou shall leave them for the poor and stranger:

I am the Lord your God. Ye shall not steal, neither deal falsely, neither lie one to another. And ye shall not swear by my name falsely, neither shall thou profane the name of thy God: I am the Lord. Thou shall not defraud thy neighbor, neither rob him: the wages of him that is hired shall not abide with thee all night until the morning. Thou shall not curse the deaf, nor put a stumbling block before the blind, but shall fear thy God: I am the Lord.

Ye shall do no unrighteousness in judgment: thou shall not respect the person of the poor, nor honor the person of the mighty: but in righteousness shall thou judge thy neighbor. Thou shall not go up and down as a talebearer among thy people: neither shall thou stand against the blood of thy neighbor. I am the Lord.

Thou shall not hate thy brother in thine heart: thou shall in any wise rebuke thy neighbor, and not suffer sin upon him. Thou shall not avenge, nor bear any grudge against the children of thy people, but thou shall love thy neighbor as thyself: **I am the Lord. Ye shall keep my Statutes.** Thou shall not let thy cattle gender with a diverse kind: thou shall not sow thy field with mingled seed: neither shall a garment mingled of linen and woolen come upon thee.

**And whosoever lieth carnally with a woman, that is a bondmaid, betrothed to a husband, and not at all redeemed, nor freedom given her; she shall be scourged; they shall not be put to death, because she was not free.** And he shall bring his trespass offering unto the Lord, unto the door of the tabernacle of the congregation, even a ram for a trespass offering.

**And the priest shall make an atonement for him with the ram of the trespass offering before the Lord for his sin which he hath done: and the sin which he hath done shall be forgiven him.** And when ye shall come into the land and shall have planted all manner of trees for food, then ye shall count the fruit thereof as uncircumcised: three years shall it be as uncircumcised unto you: it shall not be eaten of.

**But in the fourth year all the fruit thereof shall be holy to praise the Lord withal. And in the fifth year shall ye eat of the fruit thereof, that it may yield unto you the increase thereof: I am the Lord your God.**

**Ye shall not eat anything with the blood: neither shall ye use enchantment, nor observe times. Ye shall not round the corners of your heads, neither shall thou mar the corners of thy beard. Ye shall**

not make any cuttings in your flesh for the dead, nor print any marks upon you: I am the Lord.

Do not prostitute thy daughter, to cause her to be a whore; lest the land fall to whoredom, and the land become full of wickedness. Ye shall keep my Sabbaths and reverence my sanctuary: I am the Lord. Regard not them that have familiar spirits, neither seek after wizards, to be defiled by them: I am the Lord your God. Thou shall rise up before the hoary head, and honor the face of the old man, and fear thy God: I am the Lord. And if a stranger sojourn with thee in your land, ye shall not vex him.

But the stranger that dwelled with you shall be unto you as one born among you, and thou shall love him as thyself; for ye were strangers in the land of Egypt: I am the Lord your God. Ye shall do no unrighteousness in judgment, in meteyard, in weight, or in measure. Just balances, just weights, a just ephah, and a just him, shall ye have: I am the Lord your God, which brought you out of the land of Egypt. Therefore, shall ye observe all my statutes, and all my judgments, and do them: **I am the Lord.**

# LEVITICUS 20:1-27

## *Observe the Lord's Statutes*

A nd the Lord spoke unto Moses, saying, Again, thou shall say to the children of Israel, Whosoever he be of the children of Israel, or of the strangers that sojourn in Israel, that gives any of his seed unto Molech; he shall surely be put to death: the people of the land shall stone him with stones.

And I will set my face against that man and will cut him off from among his people; because he hath given of his seed unto Molech, to defile my sanctuary, and to profane my holy name. And if the people of the land do any ways hide their eyes from the man, when he gives of his seed unto Molech, and kill him not:

(This is abortion, they are steal killing babies today, this is SIN, and God is not pleased. This is shedding Innocence blood). And some people wonder why the world is in the mess, that it is in.

Sin against God's Word, it's all in the Bible, we need to pray, read and study it every day, we need to know how to live the Right way, and we need to know about the end of this World, because there will be an end.

54

# ARE YOU READY TO MEET YOUR MAKER?

························································································

## *(Life after death)*

Then I will set my face against that man, and against his family, and will cut him off, and all that go a whoring after him, to commit whoredom with Molech, from among their people. And the soul that turned after such as have familiar spirits, and after wizards, to go a whoring after them, I will even set my face against that soul, and will cut him off from among his people.

**<u>Sanctify yourselves therefore, and be ye holy: for I am the Lord your God. And ye shall keep my statutes, and do them: I am the Lord which sanctify you.</u> For everyone that cursed his father, or his mother shall be surely put to death: he hath cursed his father or his mother; his blood shall be upon him.**

**And the man that committed adultery with another man's wife, even he that committed adultery with his neighbor's wife, the adulterer and the adulteress shall surely be put to death.**

**And the man that lieth with his father's wife hath uncovered his father's nakedness: both of them shall surely be put to death; their blood shall be upon them. And if a man lies with his daughter in law, both of them shall surely be put to death: they have wrought confusion; their blood shall be upon them.**

***If a man also lies with mankind, as he lieth with a woman, both of them have committed an abomination: they shall surely be put to**

death; their blood shall be upon them. (Homosexuals and Lesbians - man with man & woman with woman)

*(And Hell followed, and they will be thrown into the Lake of Fire. This is Homosexuals, it is already written, God knows how some people are, and the devil, the deceiver, it is a shame, people don't believe God, He is the reason that we are here, He is Love. He Loves us so much, I love Him too. Do You? I pray that you do and tell others.)

And if a man takes a wife and her mother, it is wickedness: they shall be burnt with fire, both he and they; that there be no wickedness among you. And if a man lie with a beast, he shall surely be put to death: and ye shall slay the beast.

And if a woman approach unto any beast, and lie down thereto, thou shall kill the woman, and the beast: they shall surely be put to death; their blood shall be upon them.

And if a man shall take his sister, his father's daughter, or his mother's daughter, and see her nakedness, and she see his nakedness; it is a wicked thing; and they shall be cut off in the sight of their people: he hath uncovered his sister's nakedness; he shall bear his iniquity.

And if a man shall lie with a woman having her sickness and shall uncover her nakedness; he hath discovered her fountain, and she hath uncovered the fountain of her blood: and both of them shall be cut off from among their people.

And thou shall not uncover the nakedness of thy mother's sister, nor of thy father's sister: for he uncovered his near kin: they shall bear their iniquity.

And if a man shall lie with his uncle's wife, he hath uncovered his uncle's nakedness: they shall bear their sin; they shall die childless.

And if a man shall take his brother's wife, it is an unclean thing: he hath uncovered his brother's nakedness; they shall be childless.

Ye shall therefore keep all my statutes, and all my judgments, and do them: that the land, whither I bring you to dwell therein, spue you not out.

**And ye shall not walk in the manners of the nation, which I cast out before you: for they committed all these things and therefore I abhorred them. But I have said unto you.**

**Ye shall inherit their land, and I will give it unto you to possess it, a land that flowed with milk and honey: I am the Lord your God, which have separated you from other people.**

Ye shall therefore put difference between clean beasts and unclean, and between unclean fowls and clean: and ye shall not make your souls abominable by beast, or by fowl, or by any manner of living thing that crept on the ground, which I have separated from you as unclean.

**And ye shall be holy unto me: for I the Lord am holy, and have severed you from other people, that ye should be mine. A man also or woman that hath a familiar spirit, or that is a wizard, shall surely be put to death: they shall stone them with stones: their blood shall be upon them.**

# LEVITICUS 21:1-24

......................................................

## *Priests Holy to God*

And the Lord said unto Moses, Speak unto the priests the sons of Aaron, and say unto them, There shall none be defiled for the dead among his people: But for his kin, that is near unto him, that is, for his mother, and for his father, and for his son, and for his daughter, and for his brother. And for his sister a virgin, that is nigh unto him, which hath had no husband; for her may he be defiled. But he shall not defile himself, being a chief man among his people, to profane himself.

They shall not make baldness upon their head, neither shall they shave off the corner of their beard, nor make any cuttings in their flesh. They shall be holy unto their God, and not profane the name of their God: for the offerings of the Lord made by fire, and the bread of their God, they do offer: therefore, they shall be holy.

They shall not take a wife that is a whore, or profane; neither shall they take a woman put away from her husband: for he is holy unto his God. Thou shall sanctify him; therefore, for he offered the bread of thy God: he shall be holy unto thee: for I the Lord, which sanctify you, am holy. And the daughter of any priest, if she profanes herself by playing the whore, she profaned her father: she shall be burnt with fire.

And he that is the high priest among his brethren, upon whose head the anointing oil was poured, and that is consecrated to put on the garments, shall not uncover his head, nor rend his clothes; Neither

58

shall he go into any dead body, nor defile himself for his father, or for his mother;

Neither shall he go out of the sanctuary, nor profane the sanctuary of his God; for the crown of the anointing oil of his God is upon him: I am the Lord. And he shall take a wife in her virginity. A widow, or a divorced woman, or profane, or a harlot, these shall he not take: but he shall take a virgin of his own people to wife.

Neither shall he profane his seed among his people: for I the Lord do sanctify him. And the Lord spoke unto Moses, saying, Speak unto Aaron, saying, Whosoever he be of thy seed in their generations that hath any blemish, let him not approach to offer the bread of his God. For whatsoever man he be that hath a blemish, he shall not approach: a blind man, or a lame, or he that hath a flat nose, or anything superfluous, Or a man that is broken footed, or broken handed, Or crookback, or a dwarf, or that hath a blemish in his eye, or be scurvy, or scabbed, or hath his stones broken;

No man that hath a blemish of the seed of Aaron the priest shall come nigh to offer the offerings of the Lord made by fire: he hath a blemish; he shall not come nigh to offer the bread of his God. He shall eat the bread of his God, both of the most holy, and of the holy. Only he shall not go in unto the vail, nor come nigh unto the altar, because he hath a blemish; that he profanes not my sanctuaries: For I the Lord do sanctify them. And Moses told it unto Aaron, and to his sons, and unto all the children of Israel.

# LEVITICUS 22:1-33

......................................

## *Priest Holy to the Lord*

And the Lord spoke unto Moses, saying, Speak unto Aaron and to his sons, that they separate themselves from the holy things of the children of Israel, and that they profane not my holy name in those things which they hallow unto me: I am the Lord. Say unto them, Whosoever he be of all your seed among your generations, that goeth unto the holy things, which the children of Israel hallow unto the Lord, having his uncleanness upon him, that soul shall be cut off from my presence: I am the Lord.

What man so ever of the seed of Aaron is a leper, or hath a running issue; he shall not eat of the holy things, until he be clean. And whoso touched anything that is unclean by the dead, or a man whose seed goeth from him.

Or whosoever touched any creeping thing, whereby he may be made unclean, or a man of whom he may take uncleanness, whatsoever uncleanness he hath; The soul which hath touched any such shall be unclean until even, and shall not eat of the holy things, unless he washes his flesh with water.

And when the sun is down, he shall be clean, and shall afterward eat of the holy things; because it is his food. That which dieth of itself, or is torn with beasts, he shall not eat to defile himself therewith; I am the Lord. They shall therefore keep mine ordinance, lest they bear sin for it, and die therefore, if they profane it: I the Lord do sanctify them.

There shall no stranger eat of the holy thing: a sojourner of the priest, or a hired servant, shall not eat of the holy thing. But if the priest buys any soul with his money, he shall eat of it, and he that is born in his house: they shall eat of his meat.

If the priest's daughter also be married unto a stranger, she may not eat of an offering of the holy things. But if the priest's daughter be a widow, or divorced, and have no child, and is returned unto her father's house, as in her youth, she shall eat of her father's meat: but there shall no stranger eat thereof.

And if a man eats of the holy thing unwittingly, then he shall put the fifth part thereof unto it and shall give it unto the priest with the holy thing. And they shall not profane the holy things of the children of Israel, which they offer unto the Lord;

Or suffer them to bear the iniquity of trespass, when they eat their holy things: for I the Lord do sanctify them. And the Lord spoke unto Moses, saying,

Speak unto Aaron, and to his sons, and unto all the children of Israel, and say unto them, Whatsoever he be of the house of Israel, or of the strangers in Israel, that will offer his oblation for all his vows, and for all his freewill offerings, which they will offer unto the Lord for a burnt offering;

Ye shall offer at your own will a male without blemish, of the beeves, of the sheep, or of the goats. But whatsoever hath a blemish, that shall ye not offer: for it shall not be acceptable for you. And whosoever offered a sacrifice of peace offerings unto the Lord to accomplish his vow, or a freewill offering in beeves or sheep, it shall be perfect to be accepted; there shall be no blemish therein. Blind, or broken, or maimed, or having a wen, or scurvy, or scabbed, ye shall not offer these unto the Lord, nor make an offering by fire of them upon the altar unto the Lord.

Either a bullock or a lamb that hath anything superfluous or lacking in his parts, that mayest thou offer for a freewill offering; but for a vow it shall not be accepted.

Ye shall not offer unto the Lord that which is bruised, or crushed, or broken, or cut; neither shall ye make any offering thereof in your land. Neither from a stranger's hand shall ye offer the bread of your God of any of these; because their corruption is in them, and blemishes be in them: they shall not be accepted for you.

And the Lord spoke unto Moses, saying, When a bullock, or a sheep, or a goat, is brought forth, then it shall be seven days under the dam; and from the eighth day and thenceforth it shall be accepted for an offering made by fire unto the Lord. And whether it be cow, or ewe, ye shall not kill it and her young both in one day.

And when ye will offer a sacrifice of thanksgiving unto the Lord, offer it at your own will. On the same day it shall be eaten up; ye shall leave none of it until the morrow: I am the Lord. Therefore, shall ye keep My commandments, and do them: I am the Lord.

Neither shall ye profane My holy name; but I will be hallowed among the children of Israel: I am the Lord which hallow you, That brought you out of the land of Egypt, to be your God: I am the Lord.

# LEVITICUS 23:1-44

........................................

## *The Appointed Feasts*

A nd the Lord spoke unto Moses, saying, Speak unto the children of Israel, and say unto them, Concerning the feasts of the Lord, which ye shall proclaim to be holy convocations, even these are my feasts. Six days shall work be done: but the seventh day is the sabbath of rest, a holy convocation; ye shall do no work therein: it is the sabbath of the Lord in all your dwellings. These are the feasts of the Lord, even holy convocations, which ye shall proclaim in their seasons. In the fourteenth day of the first month at even is the Lord's Passover.

And on the fifteenth day of the same month is the feast of unleavened bread unto the Lord: seven days ye must eat unleavened bread. In the first day ye shall have a holy convocation: ye shall do no servile work therein. But ye shall offer an offering made by fire unto the Lord seven days: in the seventh day is a holy convocation: ye shall do no servile work therein.

And the Lord spoke unto Moses, saying, Speak unto the children of Israel, and say unto them, When ye be come into the land which I give unto you, and shall reap the harvest thereof, then ye shall bring a sheaf of the first fruits of your harvest unto the priest: And he shall wave the sheaf before the Lord, to be accepted for you: on the morrow after the sabbath the priest shall wave it.

And ye shall offer that day when ye wave the sheaf and he lamb without blemish of the first year for a burnt offering unto the Lord. And the meat offering thereof shall be two tenth deals of fine flour mingled with oil, an offering made by fire unto the Lord for a sweet savor: and the drink offering thereof shall be of wine, the fourth part of him.

And ye shall eat neither bread, nor parched corn, nor green ears, until the selfsame day that ye have brought an offering unto your God: it shall be a statute forever throughout your generations in all your dwellings. And ye shall count unto you from the morrow after the sabbath, from the day that ye brought the sheaf of the wave offering; seven sabbaths shall be complete:

Even unto the morrow after the seventh sabbath shall ye number fifty days; and ye shall offer a new meat offering unto the Lord. Ye shall bring out of your habitations two wave loaves of two tenth deals; they shall be of fine flour; they shall be baked with leaven; they are the first fruits unto the Lord.

And ye shall offer with the bread seven lambs without blemish of the first year, and one young bullock, and two rams: they shall be for a burnt offering unto the Lord, with their meat offering, and their drink offerings, even an offering made by fire, of sweet savor unto the Lord.

Then ye shall sacrifice one kid of the goats for a sin offering, and two lambs of the first year for a sacrifice of peace offerings. And the priest shall wave them with the bread of the first fruits for a wave offering before the Lord, with the two lambs: they shall be holy to the Lord for the priest. And ye shall proclaim on the selfsame day, that it may be a holy convocation unto you: ye shall do no servile work therein: it shall be a statute forever in all your dwellings throughout your generations.

And when ye reap the harvest of your land, thou shall not make clean riddance of the corners of thy field when thou reapest, neither shall thou gather any gleaning of thy harvest: thou shall leave them unto the poor, and to the stranger: I am the Lord your God.

And the Lord spoke unto Moses, saying, Speak unto the children of Israel, saying, in the seventh month, in the first day of the month, shall ye have a Sabbath, a memorial of blowing of trumpets, a holy convocation. Ye shall do no servile work therein: but ye shall offer an offering made by fire unto the Lord. And the Lord spoke unto Moses, saying, also on the tenth day of this seventh month there shall be a day of atonement: it shall be a holy convocation unto you; and ye shall afflict your souls, and offer an offering made by fire unto the Lord.

And ye shall do no work in that same day: for it is a day of atonement, to make an atonement for you before the Lord your God. For whatsoever soul it be that shall not be afflicted in that same day, he shall be cut off from among his people. And whatsoever soul it be that doeth any work in that same day, the same soul will I destroy from among his people.

Ye shall do no manner of work: it shall be a statute forever throughout your generations in all your dwellings. It shall be unto you a Sabbath of rest, and ye shall afflict your souls: in the ninth day of the month at even, from even unto even, shall ye celebrate your Sabbath.

And the Lord spoke unto Moses, saying, Speak unto the children of Israel, saying, the fifteenth day of this seventh month shall be the feast of tabernacles for seven days unto the Lord. On the first day shall be a holy convocation: ye shall do no servile work therein.

Seven days ye shall offer an offering made by fire unto the Lord: on the eighth day shall be a holy convocation unto you; and ye shall offer an offering made by fire unto the Lord: it is a solemn assembly; and ye shall do no servile work therein.

These are the feasts of the Lord, which ye shall proclaim to be holy convocations, to offer an offering made by fire unto the Lord, a burnt offering, and a meat offering, a sacrifice, and drink offerings, everything upon his day: Beside the Sabbaths of the Lord, and beside your gifts, and beside all your vows, and beside all your freewill offerings, which ye give unto the Lord.

Also, in the fifteenth day of the seventh month, when ye have gathered in the fruit of the land, ye shall keep a feast unto the Lord seven days: on the first day shall be a Sabbath, and on the eighth day shall be a Sabbath.

And ye shall take you on the first day the boughs of goodly trees, branches of palm trees, and the boughs of thick trees, and willows of the brook; and ye shall rejoice before the Lord your God seven days.

And ye shall keep it a feast unto the Lord seven days in the year. It shall be a statute forever in your generations: ye shall celebrate it in the

<u>seventh month.</u> Ye shall dwell in booths seven days; all that are Israelites born shall dwell in booths:

That your generations may know that I made the children of Israel to dwell in booths, when I brought them out of the land of Egypt: I am the Lord your God. And Moses declared unto the children of Israel the feasts of the Lord.

# LEVITICUS 24:1-23

......................................

## *Punishment of Blasphemy*

A nd the Lord spoke unto Moses, saying, Command the children of Israel, that they bring unto the pure oil olive beaten for the light, to cause the lamps to burn continually. Without the vail of the testimony, in the tabernacle of the congregation, shall Aaron order it from the evening unto the morning before the Lord continually: it shall be a statute forever in your generations.

He shall order the lamps upon the pure candlestick before the Lord continually. And thou shall take fine flour and bake twelve cakes thereof: two tenth deals shall be in one cake. And thou shall set them in two rows, six on a row, upon the pure table before the Lord. And thou shall put pure frankincense upon each row, that it may be on the bread for a memorial, even an offering made by fire unto the Lord. Every Sabbath he shall set it in order before the Lord continually, being taken from the children of Israel by an everlasting covenant.

And it shall be Aaron's and his sons'; and they shall eat it in the holy place: for it is most holy unto him of the offerings of the Lord made by fire by a perpetual statute.

And the son of an Israelitish woman, whose father was an Egyptian, went out among the children of Israel: and this son of the Israelitish woman and a man of Israel strove together in the camp; And the Israelitish woman's son blasphemed the name of the Lord, and cursed. And they brought him unto Moses: (and his mother's name was Shelomith, the daughter of Dibri, of the tribe of Dan:) And they put him in ward, that the mind of the Lord might have showed them.

And the Lord spoke unto Moses, saying, Bring forth him that hath cursed without the camp; and let all that heard him lay their hands upon his head, and let all the congregation stone him.

And thou shall speak unto the children of Israel, saying, Whosoever curses his God shall bear his sin. And he that blasphemed the name of the Lord, he shall surely be put to death, and all the congregation shall certainly stone him: as well the stranger, as he that is born in the land, when he blasphemed the name of the Lord, shall be put to death.

And he that killed any man shall surely be put to death. And he that killed a beast shall make it good; beast for beast. And if a man causes a blemish in his neighbor; as he hath done, so shall it be done to him; Breach for breach, eye for eye, tooth for tooth: as he hath caused a blemish in a man, so shall it be done to him again.

And he that killed a beast, he shall restore it: and he that killed a man, he shall be put to death. Ye shall have one manner of law, as well for the stranger, as for one of your own country: for I am the Lord your God. And Moses spoke to the children of Israel that they should bring forth him that had cursed out of the camp, and stone him with stones. And the children of Israel did as the Lord commanded Moses.

# LEVITICUS 25:1-55

....................................

## *The Redemption of Servants*

And the Lord spoke unto Moses in mount Sinai, saying, Speak unto the children of Israel, and say unto them, When ye come into the land which I give you, then shall the land keep a Sabbath unto the Lord. Six years thou shall sow thy field, and six years thou shall prune thy vineyard, and gather in the fruit thereof; But in the seventh year shall be a Sabbath of rest unto the land, a Sabbath for the Lord: thou shall neither sow thy field, nor prune thy vineyard.

That which growth of its own accord of thy harvest thou shall not reap, neither gather the grapes of thy vine undressed: for it is a year of rest unto the land. And the Sabbath of the land shall be meat for you; for thee, and for thy servant, and for thy maid, and for thy hired servant, and for thy stranger that sojourned with thee. And for thy cattle, and for the beast that are in thy land, shall all the increase thereof be meat.

And thou shall number seven Sabbaths of years unto thee, seven times seven years; and the space of the seven Sabbaths of years shall be unto thee forty and nine years. Then shall thou cause the trumpet of the jubilee to sound on the tenth day of the seventh month, in the day of atonement shall ye make the trumpet sound throughout all your land. And ye shall hallow the fiftieth year and proclaim liberty throughout all the land unto all the inhabitants thereof: it shall be a jubilee unto you; and ye shall return every man unto his possession, and ye shall return every man unto his family. A jubilee shall that fiftieth year be unto you:

ye shall not sow, neither reap that which growth of itself in it, nor gather the grapes in it of thy vine undressed.

For it is the jubilee; it shall be holy unto you: ye shall eat the increase thereof out of the field. In the year of this jubilee ye shall return every man unto his possession. And if thou sell ought unto thy neighbor, or buys ought of thy neighbor's hand, ye shall not oppress one another: According to the number of years after the jubilee thou shall buy of thy neighbor, and according unto the number of years of the fruits he shall sell unto thee:

According to the multitude of years thou shall increase the price thereof, and according to the fewness of years thou shall diminish the price of it: for according to the number of the years of the fruits doth he sells unto thee. Ye shall not therefore oppress one another; but thou shall fear thy God: for I am the Lord your God.

Wherefore ye shall do My statutes, and keep My judgments, and do them; and ye shall dwell in the land in safety. And the land shall yield her fruit, and ye shall eat your fill, and dwell therein in safety. And if ye shall say, What shall we eat the seventh year? Behold, we shall not sow, nor gather in our increase: Then I will command My blessing upon you in the sixth year, and it shall bring forth fruit for three years. And ye shall sow the eighth year and eat yet of old fruit until the ninth year; until her fruits come in ye shall eat of the old store.

The land shall not be sold for ever: for the land is Mine, for ye are strangers and sojourners with Me. And in all the land of your possession ye shall grant a redemption for the land. If thy brother be waxen poor, and hath sold away some of his possession, and if any of his kin come to redeem it, then shall he redeem that which his brother sold. And if the man has none to redeem it, and himself be able to redeem it;

Then let him count the years of the sale thereof and restore the over plus unto the man to whom he sold it; that he may return unto his possession. But if he be not able to restore it to him, then that which is sold shall remain in the hand of him that hath bought it until the year of jubilee: and in the jubilee it shall go out, and he shall return unto his possession. And if a man sells a dwelling house in a walled city, then he may redeem it within a whole year after it is sold; within a full year may he redeem it.

And if it be not redeemed within the space of a full year, then the house that is in the walled city shall be established for ever to him that bought it throughout his generations: it shall not go out in the jubilee. But the houses of the villages which have no wall round about them shall be counted as the fields of the country: they may be redeemed, and they shall go out in the jubilee. Notwithstanding the cities of the Levites, and the houses of the cities of their possession, may the Levites redeem at any time.

And if a man purchases of the Levites, then the house that was sold, and the city of his possession, shall go out in the year of jubilee: for the houses of the cities of the Levites are their possession among the children of Israel. But the field of the suburbs of their cities may not be sold; for it is their perpetual possession. And if thy brother be waxen poor and fallen in decay with thee; then thou shall relieve him: yea, though he be a stranger, or a sojourner; that he may live with thee.

<u>Take thou no usury of him or increase: but fear thy God; that thy brother may live with thee. Thou shall not give him thy money upon usury, nor lend him thy victuals for increase. I am the Lord your God,</u> which brought you forth out of the land of Egypt, to give you the land of Canaan, and to be your God.

And if thy brother that dwelled by thee be waxen poor and be sold unto thee; thou shall not compel him to serve as a bondservant: But, as a hired servant, and as a sojourner, he shall be with thee, and shall serve thee unto the year of jubilee. And then shall he depart from thee, both he and his children with him, and shall return unto his own family, and unto the possession of his fathers shall he return.

For they are my servants, which I brought forth out of the land of Egypt: they shall not be sold as bondmen. Thou shall not rule over him with rigor; but shall fear thy God. Both thy bondmen, and thy bondmaids, which thou shall have, shall be of the heathen that are round about you; of them shall ye buy bondmen and bondmaids.

Moreover, of the children of the strangers that do sojourn among you, of them shall ye buy, and of their families that are with you, which they begat in your land: and they shall be your possession. And ye shall take them as an inheritance for your children after you, to inherit them for a possession; they shall be your bondmen forever: but over your brethren the children of Israel, ye shall not rule one over another with rigor.

And if sojourner or stranger wax rich by thee, and thy brother that dwelled by him wax poor, and sell himself unto the stranger or sojourner by thee, or to the stock of the stranger's family: After that he is sold, he may be redeemed again; one of his brethren may redeem him:

Either his uncle, or his uncle's son, may redeem him, or any that is nigh of kin unto him of his family may redeem him; or if he be able, he may redeem himself. And he shall reckon with him that bought him from the year that he was sold to him unto the year of jubilee: and the price of his sale shall be according unto the number of years, according to the time of a hired servant shall it be with him.

If there be yet many years behind, according unto them he shall give again the price of his redemption out of the money that he was bought for. And if there remain but few years unto the year of jubilee, then he shall count with him, and according unto his years shall he give him again the price of his redemption. And as a yearly hired servant shall he be with him: and the other shall not rule with rigor over him in thy sight.

And if he be not redeemed in these years, then he shall go out in the year of jubilee, both he, and his children with him. For unto me the children of Israel are servants; they are my servants whom I brought forth out of the land of Egypt: I am the Lord your God.

# LEVITICUS 26:1-46

........................................

## *The Year of Jubilee*

Ye shall make you no idols nor graven image, neither rear you up a standing image, neither shall ye set up any image of stone in your land, to bow down unto it: for I am the Lord your God. Ye shall keep my Sabbaths and reverence my sanctuary: I am the Lord. If ye walk in my statutes, and keep my commandments, and do them; Then I will give you rain in due season, and the land shall yield her increase, and the trees of the field shall yield their fruit.

And your threshing shall reach unto the vintage, and the vintage shall reach unto the sowing time: and ye shall eat your bread to the full, and dwell in your land safely.

And I will give peace in the land, and ye shall lie down, and none shall make you afraid: and I will rid evil beasts out of the land, neither shall the sword go through your land. And ye shall chase your enemies, and they shall fall before you by the sword. And five of you shall chase a hundred, and a hundred of you shall put ten thousand to flight: and your enemies shall fall before you by the sword.

For I will have respect unto you, and make you fruitful, and multiply you, and establish my covenant with you.

And ye shall eat old store and bring forth the old because of the new. And I will set my tabernacle among you: and my soul shall not abhor you. And I will walk among you, and will be your God, and ye shall be my people. I am the Lord your God, which brought you forth out of the land of Egypt, that ye should not be their bondmen; and I have broken the bands of your yoke, and made you go upright.

But if ye will not hearken unto me, and will not do all these commandments; And if ye shall despise my statutes, or if your soul abhors my judgments, so that ye will not do all my commandments, but that ye break my covenant:

I also will do this unto you; I will even appoint over you terror, consumption, and the burning ague, that shall consume the eyes, and cause sorrow of heart: and ye shall sow your seed in vain, for your enemies shall eat it. And I will set my face against you, and ye shall be slain before your enemies: they that hate you shall reign over you; and ye shall flee when none pursuit you.

And if ye will not yet for all this hearken unto me, then I will punish you seven times more for your sins. And I will break the pride of your power; and I will make your heaven as iron, and your earth as brass: And your strength shall be spent in vain: for your land shall not yield her increase, neither shall the trees of the land yield their fruits.

And if ye walk contrary unto me and will not hearken unto me; I will bring seven times more plagues upon you according to your sins. I will also send wild beasts among you, which shall rob you of your children, and destroy your cattle, and make you few in number; and your highways shall be desolate.

And if ye will not be reformed by me by these things but will walk contrary unto me; Then will I also walk contrary unto you and will punish you yet seven times for your sins. And I will bring a sword upon you, that shall avenge the quarrel of my covenant: and when ye are gathered together within your cities, I will send the pestilence among you; and ye shall be delivered into the hand of the enemy.

And when I have broken the staff of your bread, ten women shall bake your bread in one oven, and they shall deliver you your bread again by weight: and ye shall eat, and not be satisfied. And if ye will not for all this hearken unto me but walk contrary unto me; Then I will walk contrary unto you also in fury; and I, even I, will chastise you seven times for your sins.

And ye shall eat the flesh of your sons, and the flesh of your daughters shall ye eat. And I will destroy your high places, and cut down your images, and cast your carcasses upon the carcasses of your idols, and my soul shall abhor you. And I will make your cities waste, and bring your sanctuaries unto desolation, and I will not smell the savor of your sweet odors.

And I will bring the land into desolation: and your enemies which dwell therein shall be astonished at it. And I will scatter you among the heathen and will draw out a sword after you: and your land shall be desolate, and your cities waste. Then shall the land enjoy her Sabbaths, as long as it lieth desolate, and ye be in your enemies' land; even then shall the land rest and enjoy her Sabbaths. As long as it lieth desolate it shall rest; because it did not rest in your Sabbaths, when ye dwelt upon it.

And upon them that are left alive of you I will send a faintness into their hearts in the lands of their enemies; and the sound of a shaken leaf shall chase them; and they shall flee, as fleeing from a sword; and they shall fall when none pursued. And they shall fall one upon another, as it were before a sword, when none pursueth: and ye shall have no power to stand before your enemies. And ye shall perish among the heathen, and the land of your enemies shall eat you up. And they that are left of you shall pine away in their iniquity in your enemies' lands; and also, in the iniquities of their fathers shall they pine away with them.

If they shall confess their iniquity, and the iniquity of their fathers, with their trespass which they trespassed against me, and that also they have walked contrary unto me; And that I also have walked contrary unto them, and have brought them into the land of their enemies; if then their uncircumcised hearts be humbled, and they then accept of the punishment of their iniquity: Then will I remember my covenant with Jacob, and also my covenant with Isaac, and also my covenant with Abraham will I remember; and I will remember the land.

The land also shall be left of them, and shall enjoy her Sabbaths, while she lieth desolate without them: and they shall accept of the punishment of their iniquity: because, even because they despised my judgments, and because their soul abhorred my statutes. And yet for all that, when they be in the land of their enemies. I will not cast them away, neither will

I abhor them, to destroy them utterly, and to break my covenant with them: for I am the Lord their God.

But I will for their sakes remember the covenant of their ancestors, whom I brought forth out of the land of Egypt in the sight of the heathen, that I might be their God: I am the Lord. These are the statutes and judgments and laws, which the Lord made between him and the children of Israel in mount Sinai by the hand of Moses.

# LEVITICUS 27:1-34

......................................

## *The Laws of Vows and Tithes*

A nd the Lord spoke unto Moses, saying, Speak unto the children of Israel, and say unto them, When a man shall make a singular vow, the persons shall be for the Lord by thy estimation. And thy estimation shall be of the male from twenty years old even unto sixty years old, even thy estimation shall be fifty shekels of silver, after the shekel of the sanctuary.

And if it be a female, then thy estimation shall be thirty shekels. And if it be from five years old even unto twenty years old, then thy estimation shall be of the male twenty shekels, and for the female ten shekels.

And if it be from a month old even unto five years old, then thy estimation shall be of the male five shekels of silver, and for the female thy estimation shall be three shekels of silver.

And if it be from sixty years old and above; if it be a male, then thy estimation shall be fifteen shekels, and for the female ten shekels. But if he be poorer than thy estimation, then he shall present himself before the priest, and the priest shall value him; according to his ability that vowed shall the priest value him.

And if it be a beast, whereof men bring an offering unto the Lord, all that any man gives of such unto the Lord shall be holy. He shall not alter it, nor change it, a good for a bad, or a bad for a good: and if he shall at all change beast for beast, then it and the exchange thereof shall be holy.

And if it be any unclean beast, of which they do not offer a sacrifice unto the Lord, then he shall present the beast before the priest: And the priest shall value it, whether it be good or bad: as thou values it, who art the priest, so shall it be. But if he will at all redeem it, then he shall add a fifth part thereof unto thy estimation.

And when a man shall sanctify his house to be holy unto the Lord, then the priest shall estimate it, whether it be good or bad: as the priest shall estimate it, so shall it stand. And if he that sanctified it will redeem his house, then he shall add the fifth part of the money of thy estimation unto it, and it shall be his.

And if a man shall sanctify unto the Lord some part of a field of his possession, then thy estimation shall be according to the seed thereof: a homer of barley seed shall be valued at fifty shekels of silver. If he sanctifies his field from the year of jubilee, according to thy estimation it shall stand. But if he sanctifies his field after the jubilee, then the priest shall reckon unto him the money according to the years that remain, even unto the year of the jubilee, and it shall be abated from thy estimation.

And if he that sanctified the field will in any wise redeem it, then he shall add the fifth part of the money of thy estimation unto it, and it shall be assured to him. And if he will not redeem the field, or if he has sold the field to another man, it shall not be redeemed any more. But the field, when it goeth out in the jubilee, shall be holy unto the Lord, as a field devoted; the possession thereof shall be the priest's.

And if a man sanctifies unto the Lord a field which he hath bought, which is not of the fields of his possession; Then the priest shall reckon unto him the worth of thy estimation, even unto the year of the jubilee: and he shall give thane estimation in that day, as a holy thing unto the Lord.

In the year of the jubilee the field shall return unto him of whom it was bought, even to him to whom the possession of the land did belong. And all thy estimations shall be according to the shekel of the sanctuary: twenty gerahs shall be the shekel. Only the firstling of the beasts, which should be the Lord's firstling, no man shall sanctify it; whether it be ox, or sheep: it is the Lord's.

And if it be of an unclean beast, then he shall redeem it according to thine estimation, and shall add a fifth part of it thereto: or if it be not redeemed, then it shall be sold according to thy estimation. Notwithstanding no devoted thing, that a man shall devote unto the Lord of all that he hath, both of man and beast, and of the field of his possession, shall be sold or redeemed: every devoted thing is most holy unto the Lord.

None devoted, which shall be devoted of men, shall be redeemed; but shall surely be put to death. And all the tithe of the land, whether of the seed of the land, or of the fruit of the tree, is the Lord's: it is holy unto the Lord. And if a man will at all redeem ought of his tithes, he shall add thereto the fifth part thereof.

**And concerning the *tithe* of the herd, or of the flock, even of whatsoever passed under the rod, the *tenth* shall be holy unto the Lord.** He shall not search whether it be good or bad, neither shall he change it: and if he changes it at all, then both it and the change thereof shall be holy; it shall not be redeemed. These are the commandments, which the Lord commanded Moses for the children of Israel in mount Sinai.

# MALACHI 3:1-18

........................................

## *Old Testament*

Behold, I will send my messenger, and he shall prepare the way before me: and the Lord, whom ye seek, shall suddenly come to his temple, even the messenger of the covenant, whom ye delight in: behold, he shall come, said the Lord of hosts. But who may abide the day of his coming? And who shall stand when he appeared? For he is like a refiner's fire, and like fullers' soap:

And he shall sit as a refiner and purifier of silver: and he shall purify the sons of Levi, and purge them as gold and silver, that they may offer unto the Lord an offering in righteousness. Then shall the offering of Judah and Jerusalem be pleasant unto the Lord, as in the days of old, and as in former years.

And I will come near to you to judgment; and I will be a swift witness against the sorcerers, and against the adulterers, and against false swearers, and against those that oppress the hireling in his wages, the widow, and the fatherless, and that turn aside the stranger from his right, and fear not me, said the Lord of hosts. *For I am the Lord, I change not; therefore, ye sons of Jacob are not consumed.*

*Even from the days of your fathers ye are gone away from mine ordinances and have not kept them. Return unto me, and I will return unto you, said the Lord of hosts. But ye said, Where in shall we return?*

*Will a man rob God? Yet ye have robbed me. But ye say, Wherein have we robbed thee? In tithes and offerings. Ye are cursed with a curse: for ye have robbed me, even this whole nation. Bring ye all the tithes into the storehouse, that there may be meat in mine house, and prove me now here with, said the Lord of hosts, if I will not open you the windows of heaven, and pour you out a blessing, that there shall not be room enough to receive it.*

*\*And I will rebuke the devourer for your sakes, and he shall not destroy the fruits of your ground; neither shall your vine cast her fruit before the time in the field, said the Lord of hosts. \*And all nations shall call you blessed: for ye shall be a delightsome land, said the Lord of hosts. \*Your words have been stout against me, said the Lord. \*Yet ye say, What have we spoken so much against thee? \*Ye have said, It is vain to serve God: and what profit is it that we have kept his ordinance, and that we have walked mournfully before the Lord of hosts?*

*\*And now we call the proud happy; yea, they that work wickedness are set up; yea, they that tempt God are even delivered. \*Then they that feared the Lord spoke often one to another: and the Lord hearkened, and heard it, and a book of remembrance was written before him for them that feared the Lord, and that thought upon his name.*

*\*And they shall be mine, said the Lord of hosts, in that day when I make up my jewels; and I will spare them, as a man spare his own son that serve him. \*Then shall ye return, and discern between the righteous and the wicked, between him that serve God and him that served him not.*

**Looking at all the things that people do, and the things going on in the World, the news, we need God to help us, the People every body, I ask God for something I could do to add to my prayers and going out talking to People about Him when I was able to go. Also living the Life according to His Holy Word, the Bible. And accepting God's Son the Lord Jesus Christ, My Lord, God Bless You.**

*This idea came to me, because I had been praying for something to get the Word of God out to the unbeliever that don't live by the Word, and don't really believe that there is Life after death, I know that the Bible is True God sent Jesus for us, our Sin to be forgiven and we will have a chance to repent and go back home to be with God the Father and the Lord Jesus Christ, who came and took the punishment for us.*

*I want you to know God's will for us. I love and pray for you, even if I don't know your name, God know who you are, you are my brother or sister, God is the Father, I hope you think about your life and where you will spend Eternity. I hope it is in Heaven, don't go to Hell it's no party. I pray this book be a blessing to your life, and many others, tell someone. I Love you with the love of the Lord come back to God if you haven't!*

___An addition to this book conformation:___ *More we need to know for this life we live in Jesus Christ. I thought I was finished. I was giving more to add to this book. It is Good, we need conformation sometimes, mainly for the unbelievers, I thank God...Read along with me! Read this book again, until you understand: Wisdom!!!*

*You and I will be more blessed when we read and obey the word of God: Jehovah the Father and Jesus Christ the Son. And if we let the Holy Spirit lead and guide us. We will all be in Heaven with the Lord God Almighty, the Father, King of kings and Lord of lords, when we pass away from this Life on Earth.*

### ___Life After Death is Real.___

### ___Revelation 1:3___ = Blessed is he (or she) that reads, and they that hear the words of this prophecy, and keep those things which are written therein: for the time is at hand.

*Only if you have accepted Gods Son, and living according to His Precious Word, Jesus is the Word make flesh, came to show us the way back to God.*

### ___Heaven or Hell___
### ___Where will you spend Eternity?___
### ___[The choice is Yours]___

# LEVITICUS 1:1-27

*'Old and New'*
*"Conformation Scriptures Old to New"*

**Leviticus 1:3**= If his offering be a burnt sacrifice of the herd, let him offer a male without blemish: he shall offer it of his own voluntary will at the door of the tabernacle of the congregation before the Lord.

**Ephesians 5:27**= That he might present it to himself a glorious church, not having spot, or wrinkle, or any such thing; but that it should be holy and without blemish.

**Hebrews 9:14**= How much more shall the blood of Christ, who through the eternal Spirit offered himself without spot to God, purge your conscience from dead works to serve the living God?

**1 Peter 1:19**= But with the precious blood of Christ, as of a lamb without blemish and without spot:

**Leviticus 1:4**= And he shall put his hand upon the head of the burnt offering; and it shall be accepted for him to make atonement for him.

**Romans 12:1**= I beseech you therefore, brethren, by the mercies of God, that ye present your bodies a living sacrifice, holy, acceptable unto God, which is your reasonable service.

**Philippians 4:18**= But I have all, and abound I am full, having received of Epaphroditus the things which were sent from you, an odor of a sweet smell, a sacrifice acceptable, well pleasing to God.

**Leviticus 1:5**= And he shall kill the bullock before the Lord: and the priests, Aaron's sons, shall bring the blood, and sprinkle the blood round about upon the altar that is by the door of the tabernacle of the congregation.

**Hebrews 12:24**= And to Jesus the mediator of the new covenant, and to the blood of sprinkling, that speak better things than that of Abel.

**1 Peter 1:2**= Elect according to the foreknowledge of God the Father, through sanctification of the spirit, unto obedience and sprinkling of the blood of Jesus Christ: Grace unto you, and peace, be multiplied.

**Leviticus 1:9** = But his inwards and his legs shall he wash in water: and the priest shall burn all on the altar, to be a burnt sacrifice, an offering made by fire, of a sweet savor unto the Lord.

**2 Corinthians 2:15**= For we are unto God a sweet savor of Christ, in them that are saved, and in them that perish:

**Ephesians 5:2** =And walk in love, as Christ also hath loved us, and hath given himself for us an offering and a sacrifice to God for a sweet-smelling savor.

**Philippians. 4:18**= But I have all and abound. I am full, having received of Epaphroditus the things which were sent from you, an odor of a sweet smell, a sacrifice acceptable, well pleasing to God.

**Leviticus 1:10**= And if his offering be of the flocks, namely, of the sheep, or of the goats, for a burnt sacrifice; he shall bring it a male without blemish.

**1 Peter 1:19**= But with the precious blood of Christ, as of a lamb without blemish and without spot:

**Leviticus 1:14**= And if the burnt sacrifice for his offering to the Lord be of fowls, then he shall bring his offering of turtledoves, or of young pigeons.

**Luke 2:24**= And to offer a sacrifice according to that which is said in the law of the Lord, A pair of turtledoves, or two young pigeons.

**Leviticus 2:2**= And he shall bring it to Aaron's sons the priests: and he shall take there out his handful of the flour thereof, and of the oil thereof, with all the frankincense thereof; and the priest shall burn the memorial of it upon the altar, to be an offering made by fire, of a sweet savor unto the Lord:

**Acts 10:4**= And when he looked on him, he was afraid, and said, What is it, Lord? And he said unto him, Thy prayers and your alms are come up for a memorial before God.

**Leviticus 2:11**= No meat offering, which ye shall bring unto the Lord, shall be made with leaven: for ye shall burn no leaven, nor any honey, in any offering of the Lord made by fire.

**Matthew 16:12**= Then understood they how that he bade them not beware of the leaven of bread, but of the doctrine of the Pharisees and of the Sadducees.

**Mark 8:15**= And he charged them, saying, Take heed, beware of the leaven of the Pharisees, and of the leaven of Herod.

**Luke 12:1**= In the meantime, when there were gathered together an innumerable multitude of people, insomuch that they trode one upon another, he began to say unto his disciples first of all, Beware ye of the leaven of the Pharisees, which is hypocrisy.

**1 Corinthians 5:8**= Therefore let us keep the feast, not with old leaven, neither with the leaven of malice and wickedness; but with the unleavened bread of sincerity and truth.

**Galatians 5:9**= A little leaven leavened the whole lump.

**Leviticus 2:13**= And every oblation of thy meat offering shalt thou season with salt; neither shalt thou suffer the salt of the covenant of thy God to be lacking from thy meat offering: with all thine offerings thou shalt offer salt.

**Mark 9:49-50**= *For everyone shall be salted with fire, and every sacrifice shall be salted with salt. *Salt is good: but if the salt has lost his saltiness, wherewith will ye season it? Have salt in yourselves and have peace one with another.

**Colossians 4:6**= Let your speech be always with grace, seasoned with salt, that ye may know how ye ought to answer every man.

**Leviticus 3:17**= It shall be a perpetual statute for your generations throughout all your dwellings, that ye eat neither fat nor blood.

**Acts 15:20**= But that we write unto them, that they abstain from pollutions of idols, and from fornication, and from things strangled, and from blood.

**1 Corinthians 8:7**= Howbeit there is not in every man that knowledge: for some with conscience of the idol unto this hour eat it as a thing offered unto an idol; and their conscience being weak is defiled.

**1 Corinthians 10:7**= Neither be ye idolaters, as were some of them; as it is written, The people sat down to eat and drink, and rose up to play.

**Leviticus 4:2**= Speak unto the children of Israel, saying, If a soul shall sin through ignorance against any of the commandments of the Lord concerning things which ought not to be done, and shall do against any of them:

**Acts 3:17**= And now, brethren, I wot that through ignorance ye did it, as did also your rulers.

**Hebrews 9:7**= But into the second went the high priest alone once every year, not without blood, which he offered for himself, and for the errors of the people:

**Leviticus 4:11**= And the skin of the bullock, and all his flesh, with his head, and with his legs, and his inwards, and his dung,

**Hebrews 13:11**= For the bodies of those beasts, whose blood is brought into the sanctuary by the high priest for sin, are burned without the camp.

**Leviticus 4:12**= Even the whole bullock shall he carry forth without the camp unto a clean place, where the ashes are poured out, and burn him on the wood with fire: where the ashes are poured out shall he be burnt.

**Hebrews 13:11-12**= For the bodies of those beasts, whose blood is brought into the sanctuary by the high priest for sin, are burned without the camp. Wherefore Jesus also, that he might sanctify the people with his own blood, suffered without the gate.

**Leviticus 4:16**= And the priest that is anointed shall bring of the bullock's blood to the tabernacle of the congregation:

**Hebrews 9:12-14**= Neither by the blood of goats and calves, but by his own blood he entered in once into the holy place, having obtained eternal redemption for us. For if the blood of bulls and of goats, and the ashes of a heifer sprinkling the unclean, sanctified to the purifying of the flesh: How much more shall the blood of Christ, who through the eternal Spirit offered himself without spot to God, purge your conscience from dead works to serve the living God?

**Leviticus 5:4**= Or if a soul swear, pronouncing with his lips to do evil, or to do good, whatsoever it be that a man shall pronounce with an oath, and it be hid from him; when he know of it, then he shall be guilty in one of these.

**Acts 23:12**= And when it was day, certain of the Jews banded together, and bound themselves under a curse, saying that they would neither eat nor drink till they had killed Paul.

**Matthew 5:33-37**= Again, ye have heard that it hath been said by them of old time, Thou shall not forswear thyself, but shall perform unto the Lord your oaths: But I say unto you, Swear not at all; neither by heaven; for it is God's throne: Nor by the earth; for it is his footstool: neither by Jerusalem; for it is the city of the great King. Neither shall thou swear by thy head, because thou canst not make one hair white or black. But let your communication be, Yea, yea; Nay, nay: for whatsoever is more than these cometh of evil.

**Mark 6:23**= And he swore unto her, Whatsoever thou shall ask of me, I will give it thee, unto the half of my kingdom.

**James 5:12**= But above all things, my brethren, swear not, neither by heaven, neither by the earth, neither by any other oath: but let your yea be yea; and your nay, nay; lest ye fall into condemnation.

**Leviticus 5:7**= And if he be not able to bring a lamb, then he shall bring for his trespass, which he hath committed, two turtledoves, or two young pigeons, unto the Lord; one for a sin offering, and the other for a burnt offering.

**Luke 2:24**= And to offer a sacrifice according to that which is said in the law of the Lord, A pair of turtledoves, or two young pigeons.

**Leviticus 6:2**= If a soul sin, and commit a trespass against the Lord, and lie unto his neighbor in that which was delivered him to keep, or in fellowship, or in a thing taken away by violence, or hath deceived his neighbor.

**Acts 5:4**= Whiles it remained, was it not your own? and after it was sold, was it not in your own power? why hast thou conceived this thing in your heart? thou hast not lied unto men, but unto God.

**Colossians 3:9**= Lie not one to another, seeing that ye have put off the old man with his deeds.

**Leviticus 6:18**= All the males among the children of Aaron shall eat of It. It shall be a statute forever in your generations concerning the offerings of the Lord made by fire: every one that touched them shall be holy.

**1 Corinthians 9:13**= Do ye not know that they which minister about holy things live of the things of the temple? and they which wait at the altar are partakers with the altar?

**Leviticus 6:30**= And no sin offering, where of any of the blood is brought into the tabernacle of the congregation to reconcile withal in the holy place, shall be eaten: it shall be burnt in the fire.

**Hebrews 13:11-12**= For the bodies of those beasts, whose blood is brought into the sanctuary by the high priest for sin, are burned without the camp. Wherefore Jesus also, that he might sanctify the people with his own blood, suffered without the gate.

**Leviticus 7:20**= But the soul that eat of the flesh of the sacrifice of peace offerings, that pertain unto the Lord, having his uncleanness upon him, even that soul shall be cut off from his people.

**Hebrews 2:17**= Wherefore in all things it behooved him to be made like unto his brethren, that he might be a merciful and faithful high priest in things pertaining to God, to make reconciliation for the sins of the people.

**1 Corinthians 11:28=** But let a man examine himself, and so let him eat of that bread, and drink of that cup.

**Leviticus 7:26=** Moreover ye shall eat no manner of blood, whether it be of fowl or of beast, in any of your dwellings.

**John 6:53=** Then Jesus said unto them, Verily, verily, I say unto you, Except ye eat the flesh of the Son of man, and drink his blood, ye have no life in you.

**Acts 10:14=** But Peter said, Not so, Lord; for I have never eaten anything that is common or unclean.

**Acts 15:20=** But that we write unto them, that they abstain from pollutions of idols, and from fornication, and from things strangled, and from blood.

**Acts 15:29=** That ye abstain from meats offered to idols, and from blood, and from things strangled, and from fornication: from which if ye keep yourselves, ye shall do well. Fare ye well.

**Leviticus 8:6=** And Moses brought Aaron and his sons and washed them with water.

**Hebrews 10:22=** Let us draw near with a true heart in full assurance of faith, having our hearts sprinkled from an evil conscience, and our bodies washed with pure water.

**Leviticus 8:15=** And he slew it; and Moses took the blood and put it upon the horns of the altar roundabout with his finger, and purified the altar, and poured the blood at the bottom of the altar, and sanctified it, to make reconciliation upon it.

**Hebrews 9:22=** And almost all things are by the law purged with blood; and without shedding of blood is no remission.

**Leviticus 8:24=** And he brought Aaron's sons, and Moses put of the blood upon the tip of their right ear, and upon the thumbs of their right hands, and upon the great toes of their right feet: and Moses sprinkled the blood upon the altar round about.

**Hebrews 9:13-14=** For if the blood of bulls and of goats, and the ashes of a heifer sprinkling the unclean, sanctified to the purifying of the flesh: *How much more shall the blood of Christ, who through the eternal Spirit offered himself without spot to God, purge your conscience from dead works to serve the living God?

**Hebrews 9:18-23**= Where upon neither the first testament was dedicated without blood. For when Moses had spoken every precept to all the people according to the law, he took the blood of calves and of goats, with water, and scarlet wool, and hyssop, and sprinkled both the book, and all the people, saying, This is the blood of the testament which God hath enjoined unto you. Moreover, he sprinkled with blood both the tabernacle, and all the vessels of the ministry. And almost all things are by the law purged with blood; and without shedding of blood is no remission. It was therefore necessary that the patterns of things in the heavens should be purified with these; but the heavenly things themselves with better sacrifices than these.

**Leviticus 8:34**= As he hath done this day, so the Lord hath commanded to do, to make an atonement for you.

**Hebrews 7:16**= Who is made, not after the law of a carnal commandment, but after the power of an endless life.

**Leviticus 9:7**= And Moses said unto Aaron, Go unto the altar, and offer thy sin offering, and thy burnt offering, and make an atonement for thyself, and for the people: and offer the offering of the people, and make an atonement for them; as the Lord commanded.

**Hebrews 5:1-2**= For every high priest taken from among men is ordained for men in things pertaining to God, that he may offer both gifts and sacrifices for sins: Who can have compassion on the ignorant, and on them that are out of the way; for that he himself also is compassed with infirmity.

**Hebrews 5:3-5**= And by reason hereof he ought, as for the people, so also for himself, to offer for sins. And no man takes this honor unto himself, but he that is called of God, as was Aaron. So also, Christ glorified not himself to be made a high priest; but he that said unto him, Thou art my Son, today have I begotten thee.

**Hebrews 7:27**= Who needed not daily, as those high priests, to offer up sacrifice, first for his own sins, and then for the people's: for this he did once, when he offered up himself.

**Leviticus 9:15**= And he brought the people's offering, and took the goat, which was the sin offering for the people, and slew it, and offered it for sin, as the first.

**Hebrews 2:17**= Wherefore in all things it behooved him to be made like unto his brethren, that he might be a merciful and faithful high priest in things pertaining to God, to make reconciliation for the sins of the people.

**Hebrews 5:3**= And by reason hereof he ought, as for the people, so also for himself, to offer for sins.

**Leviticus 9:22**= And Aaron lifted up his hand toward the people, and blessed them, and came down from offering of the sin offering, and the burnt offering, and peace offerings.

**Luke 24:50**= And he led them out as far as to Bethany, and he lifted up his hands, and blessed them.

**Leviticus 10:2**= And there went out fire from the Lord, and devoured them, and they died before the Lord.

**Revelation 20:9**= And they went up on the breadth of the earth, and compassed the camp of the saints about, and the beloved city: and fire came down from God out of heaven and devoured them.

**Leviticus 10:3**= Then Moses said unto Aaron, This is it that the LORD spake, saying, I will be sanctified in them that come nigh me, and before all the people I will be glorified. And Aaron held his peace.

**John 13:31-32**= *Therefore, when he was gone out, Jesus said, Now is the Son of man glorified, and God is glorified in him. *If God be glorified in him, God shall also glorify him in himself, and shall straightway glorify him.

**2 Thessalonians 1:10**= When he shall come to be glorified in his saints, and to be admired in all of them that believe (because our testimony among you was believed) in that day.

**Leviticus 10:4**= And Moses called Mishael and Elzaphan, the sons of Uzziel the uncle of Aaron, and said unto them, Come near, carry your brethren from before the sanctuary out of the camp.

**Acts 5:6**= And the young men arose, wound him up, and carried him out, and buried him.

**Acts 5:10**= Then fell she down straightway at his feet and yielded up the ghost: and the young men came in, and found her dead, and, carrying her forth, buried her by her husband.

**Leviticus 10:9**= Do not drink wine nor strong drink, thou, nor thy sons with thee, when ye go into the tabernacle of the congregation, lest ye die: it shall be a statute forever throughout your generations:

**Luke 1:15**= For he shall be great in the sight of the Lord and shall drink neither wine nor strong drink; and he shall be filled with the Holy Ghost, even from his mother's womb.

**Ephesians 5:18**= And be not drunk with wine, wherein is excess; but be filled with the Spirit;

**1 Timothy 3:3**= Not given to wine, no striker, not greedy of filthy lucre; but patient, not a brawler, not covetous;

**Titus 1:7**= For a bishop must be blameless, as the steward of God; not self willed, not soon angry, not given to wine, no striker, not given to filthy lucre;

**Leviticus 11:2**= Speak unto the children of Israel, saying, These are the beasts which ye shall eat among all the beasts that are on the earth.

**Matthew 15:11**= Not that which goes into the mouth defiled a man; but that which cometh out of the mouth, this defiled a man.

**Acts 10:12**= Wherein were all manner of four-footed beasts of the earth, and wild beasts, and creeping things, and fowls of the air.

**Acts 10:14**= But Peter said, Not so, Lord; for I have never eaten anything that is common or unclean.

**Romans 14:14**= I know, and am persuaded by the Lord Jesus, that there is nothing unclean of itself: but to him that esteemed anything to be unclean, to him it is unclean.

**Hebrews 9:10**= Which stood only in meats and drinks, and divers washings, and carnal ordinances, imposed on them until the time of reformation.

**Hebrews 13:9**= Be not carried about with divers and strange doctrines. For it is a good thing that the heart be established with grace; not with meats, which have not profited them that have been occupied therein.

**Leviticus 11:4**= Nevertheless these shall ye not eat of them that chew the cud, or of them that divide the hoof: as the camel, because he chewed the cud, but divided not the hoof; he is unclean unto you.

**Acts 10:14**= But Peter said, Not so, Lord; for I have never eaten anything that is common or unclean.

**Leviticus 11:7**= And the swine, though he divides the hoof, and be cloven-footed, yet he chewed not the cud; he is unclean to you.

**Mark 5:1-17**= And they came over unto the other side of the sea, into the country of the Gadarenes. *And when he was come out of the ship, immediately there met him out of the tombs a man with an unclean spirit, *Who had his dwelling among the tombs; and no man could bind him, no, not with chains: Because that he had been often bound with fetters and chains, and the chains had been plucked asunder by him, and the fetters broken in pieces: neither could any man tame him. And always, night and day, he was in the mountains, and in the tombs, crying, and cutting himself with stones.

But when he saw Jesus afar off, he ran and worshipped him, And cried with a loud voice, and said, What have I to do with thee, Jesus, thou Son of the most high God? I adjure thee by God, that thou torment me not. For he said unto him, Come out of the man, thou unclean spirit. And he asked him, What is thy name? *And he answered, saying, My name is Legion: for we are many.

And he besought him much that he would not send them away out of the country. Now there was there nigh unto the mountains a great herd of swine feeding. *And all the devils besought him, saying, Send us into the swine, that we may enter into them.

*And forthwith Jesus gave them leave. And the unclean spirits went out, and entered into the swine: and the herd ran violently down a steep place into the sea, (they were about two thousand;) and were choked in the sea. *And they that fed the swine fled, and told it in the city, and in the country. And they went out to see what it was that was done. *And they come to Jesus, and see him that was possessed with the devil, and had the legion, sitting, and clothed, and in his right mind: and they were afraid. *And they that saw it told them how it befell to him that was possessed with the devil, and also concerning the swine. *And they began to pray him to depart out of their coasts.

**Leviticus 11:8**= Of their flesh shall ye not eat, and their carcase shall ye not touch; they are unclean to you.

**Mark 7:2, 15, 18**= And when they saw some of his disciples eat bread with defiled, that is to say, with unwashed, hands, they found fault. There is nothing from without a man, that entering into him can defile him: but the things which come out of him, those are they that defile the man. And he said unto them, Are ye so without understanding also? Do ye not perceive, that whatsoever thing from without entered into the man, it cannot defile him;

**Acts 10:14-15**= But Peter said, Not so, Lord; for I have never eaten anything that is common or unclean. And the voice spoke unto him again the second time, What God hath cleansed, that call not thou common.

**Acts 15:29**= That ye abstain from meats offered to idols, and from blood, and from things strangled, and from fornication: from which if ye keep yourselves, ye shall do well. Fare ye well.

**Hebrews 9:10**= Which stood only in meats and drinks, and divers washings, and carnal ordinances, imposed on them until the time of reformation.

**Leviticus 11:22**= Even these of them ye may eat; the locust after his kind, and the bald locust after his kind, and the beetle after his kind, and the grasshopper after his kind.

**Matthew 3:4**= And the same John had his raiment of camel's hair, and a leathern girdle about his loins; and his meat was locusts and wild honey.

**Mark 1:6**= And John was clothed with camel's hair, and with a girdle of a skin about his loins; and he did eat locusts and wild honey;

**Leviticus 11:25**= And whosoever bear ought of the carcass of them shall wash his clothes and be unclean until the even.

**Hebrews 9:10**= Which stood only in meats and drinks, and divers washings, and carnal ordinances, imposed on them until the time of reformation.

**Hebrews 10:22**= Let us draw near with a true heart in full assurance of faith, having our hearts sprinkled from an evil conscience, and our bodies washed with pure water.

**Revelation 7:14**= And I said unto him, Sir, thou knows. And he said to me, These are they which came out of great tribulation, and have washed their robes, and made them white in the blood of the Lamb.

**Leviticus 11:33**= And every earthen vessel, where into any of them falleth, whatsoever is in it shall be unclean; and ye shall break it.

**2 Timothy 2:21**= If a man therefore purge himself from these, he shall be a vessel unto honor, sanctified, and meet for the master's use, and prepared unto every good work.

**Revelation 2:27**= And he shall rule them with a rod of iron; as the vessels of a potter shall they be broken to shivers: even as I received of my Father.

**Leviticus 11:44-45**= For I am the Lord your God: ye shall therefore sanctify yourselves, and ye shall be holy; for I am holy: neither shall ye defile yourselves with any manner of creeping thing that creep upon the earth. For I am the Lord that bring you up out of the land of Egypt, to be your God: ye shall therefore be holy, for I am holy.

**Matthew 5:48**= Be ye therefore perfect, even as your Father which is in heaven is perfect.

**1 Thessalonians 4:7**= For God hath not called us unto uncleanness, but unto holiness.

**1 Peter 1:15-16**= But as he which hath called you is holy, so be ye holy in all manner of conversation; Because it is written, Be ye holy; for I am holy.

**Revelation 22:11, 14**= He that is unjust, let him be unjust still: and he which is filthy, let him be filthy still: and he that is righteous, let him be righteous still: and he that is holy, let him be holy still. Blessed are they that do his commandments, that they may have right to the tree of life and may enter in through the gates into the city.

**Leviticus 12:6**= And when the days of her purifying are fulfilled, for a son, or for a daughter, she shall bring a lamb of the first year for a burnt offering, and a young pigeon, or a turtledove, for a sin offering, unto the door of the tabernacle of the congregation, unto the priest:

**Luke 2:22**= And when the days of her purification according to the law of Moses were accomplished, they brought him to Jerusalem, to present him to the Lord;

**Leviticus 12:8**= And if she be not able to bring a lamb, then she shall bring two turtles, or two young pigeons; the one for the burnt offering, and the other for a sin offering: and the priest shall make an atonement for her, and she shall be clean.

**Luke 2:24**= And to offer a sacrifice according to that which is said in the law of the Lord, A pair of turtledoves, or two young pigeons.

**Leviticus 13:16**= Or if the raw flesh turns again, and be changed unto white, he shall come unto the priest;

**Luke 5:12-14**= And it came to pass, when he was in a certain city, behold a man full of leprosy: who seeing Jesus fell on his face, and besought him, saying, Lord, if thou wilt, thou canst make me clean. And he put forth his hand, and touched him, saying, I will: be thou clean. And immediately the leprosy departed from him. And he charged him to tell no man: but go, and show thyself to the priest, and offer for thy cleansing, according as Moses commanded, for a testimony unto them.

**Leviticus 13:46=** All the days wherein the plague shall be in him he shall be defiled; he is unclean: he shall dwell alone; without the camp shall his habitation be.

**Luke 17:12=** And as he entered into a certain village, there met him ten men that were lepers, which stood afar off:

**Leviticus 14:2=** This shall be the law of the leper in the day of his cleansing: He shall be brought unto the priest:

**Matthew 8:4=** And Jesus said unto him, See thou tell no man; but go thy way, show thyself to the priest, and offer the gift that Moses commanded, for a testimony unto them.

**Mark 1:40-45=** And there came a leper to him, beseeching him, and kneeling down to him, and saying unto him, If thou wilt, thou canst make me clean. And Jesus, moved with compassion, put forth his hand, and touched him, and said unto him, I will; be thou clean. And as soon as he had spoken, immediately the leprosy departed from him, and he was cleansed. And he straitly charged him, and forthwith sent him away; And said unto him, See thou say nothing to any man: but go thy way, show thyself to the priest, and offer for thy cleansing those things which Moses commanded, for a testimony unto them. But he went out, and began to publish it much, and to blaze abroad the matter, insomuch that Jesus could no more openly enter into the city but was without in desert places: and they came to him from every quarter.

**Luke 5:12-14=** And it came to pass, when he was in a certain city, behold a man full of leprosy: who seeing Jesus fell on his face, and besought him, saying, Lord, if thou wilt, thou canst make me clean. And he put forth his hand, and touched him, saying, I will: be thou clean. And immediately the leprosy departed from him. And he charged him to tell no man: but go, and show thyself to the priest, and offer for thy cleansing, according as Moses commanded, for a testimony unto them.

**Luke 17:12-14=** And as he entered into a certain village, there met him ten men that were lepers, which stood afar off: And they lifted up their voices, and said, Jesus, Master, have mercy on us. And when he saw them, he said unto them, Go show yourselves unto the priests. And it came to pass, that, as they went, they were cleansed.

**Leviticus 14:10**= And on the eighth day he shall take two he lambs without blemish, and one ewe lamb of the first year without blemish, and three tenth deals of fine flour for a meat offering, mingled with oil, and one log of oil.

**Matthew 8:4**= And Jesus said unto him, See thou tell no man; but go thy way, show thyself to the priest, and offer the gift that Moses commanded, for a testimony unto them.

**Mark 1:44**= And said unto him, See thou say nothing to any man: but go thy way, show thyself to the priest, and offer for thy cleansing those things which Moses commanded, for a testimony unto them.

**Luke 5:14**= And he charged him to tell no man: but go, and show thyself to the priest, and offer for thy cleansing, according as Moses commanded, for a testimony unto them.

**Leviticus 15:25**= And immediately he rose up before them, and took up that whereon he lay, and departed to his own house, glorifying God.

**Matthew 9:20**= And, behold, a woman, which was diseased with an issue of blood twelve years, came behind him, and touched the hem of his garment:

**Mark 5:25**= And a certain woman, which had an issue of blood twelve years,

**Luke 8:43-44**= And a woman having an issue of blood twelve years, which had spent all her living upon physicians, neither could be healed of any, Came behind him, and touched the border of his garment: and immediately her issue of blood stanched.

**Leviticus 16:2**= And the Lord said unto Moses, Speak unto Aaron thy brother, that he come not at all times into the holy place within the vail before the mercy seat, which is upon the ark; that he die not: for I will appear in the cloud upon the mercy seat.

**Hebrews 9:25**= Nor yet that he should offer himself often, as the high priest entereth into the holy place every year with blood of others;

**Leviticus 16:6=** And Aaron shall offer his bullock of the sin offering, which is for himself, and make an atonement for himself, and for his house.

**Hebrews 5:1-3=** For every high priest taken from among men is ordained for men in things pertaining to God, that he may offer both gifts and sacrifices for sins: Who can have compassion on the ignorant, and on them that are out of the way; for that he himself also is compassed with infirmity. And by reason hereof he ought, as for the people, so also for himself, to offer for sins.

**Hebrews 7:27-28=** Who needed not daily, as those high priests, to offer up sacrifice, first for his own sins, and then for the people's: for this he did once, when he offered up himself. *For the law makes men high priests which have infirmity; but the word of the oath, which was since the law, makes the Son, who is consecrated for evermore.

**Hebrews 9:7=** But into the second went the high priest alone once every year, not without blood, which he offered for himself, and for the errors of the people:

**Leviticus 16:11=** And Aaron shall bring the bullock of the sin offering, which is for himself, and shall make an atonement for himself, and for his house, and shall kill the bullock of the sin offering which is for himself:

**Hebrews 9:7=** But into the second went the high priest alone once every year, not without blood, which he offered for himself, and for the errors of the people:

**Leviticus 16:15=** Then shall he kill the goat of the sin offering, that is for the people, and bring his blood within the vail, and do with that blood as he did with the blood of the bullock, and sprinkle it upon the mercy seat, and before the mercy seat:

**Hebrews 6:19=** Which hope we have as an anchor of the soul, both sure and steadfast, and which entered into that within the veil;

**Hebrews 9:3, 7, 12 =** And after the second veil, the tabernacle which is called the Holiest of all; *But into the second went the high priest alone once every year, not without blood, which he offered for himself, and for the errors of the people: *Neither by the blood of goats and calves, but by his own blood he entered in once into the holy place, having obtained eternal redemption for us.

**Leviticus 16:16**= And he shall make an atonement for the holy place, because of the uncleanness of the children of Israel, and because of their transgressions in all their sins: and so shall he do for the tabernacle of the congregation, that remained among them in the midst of their uncleanness.

**Hebrews 2:17**= Wherefore in all things it behooved him to be made like unto his brethren, that he might be a merciful and faithful high priest in things pertaining to God, to make reconciliation for the sins of the people.

**Leviticus 16:34**= And this shall be an everlasting statute unto you, to make an atonement for the children of Israel for all their sins once a year. And he did as the Lord commanded Moses.

**Hebrews 9:7**= But into the second went the high priest alone once every year, not without blood, which he offered for himself, and for the errors of the people:

**Leviticus 17:7**= And they shall no more offer their sacrifices unto devils, after whom they have gone a whoring. This shall be a statute forever unto them throughout their generations.

**1 Corinthians 10:20**= But I say, that the things which the Gentiles sacrifice, they sacrifice to devils, and not to God: and I would not that ye should have fellowship with devils.

**Leviticus 17:11**= For the life of the flesh is in the blood: and I have given it to you upon the altar to make an atonement for your souls: for it is the blood that makes an atonement for the soul.

**Hebrews 9:22**= And almost all things are by the law purged with blood; and without shedding of blood is no remission.

**Leviticus 18:5**= Ye shall therefore keep my statutes, and my judgments: which if a man do, he shall live in them: I am the Lord.

**Luke 10:28**= And he said unto him, Thou hast answered right: this do, and thou shall live.

**Romans 10:5**= For Moses described the righteousness, which is of the law, That the man which doeth those things shall live by them.

**Galatians 3:12**= And the law is not of faith: but the man that doeth them shall live in them.

**Leviticus 18:20**= Moreover thou shall not lie carnally with thy neighbor's wife, to defile thyself with her.

**Matthew 5:27-28**= Ye have heard that it was said by them of old time, Thou shall not commit adultery: But I say unto you, That whosoever looked on a woman to lust after her hath committed adultery with her already in his heart.

**1 Corinthians 6:9**= Know ye not that the unrighteous shall not inherit the kingdom of God? Be not deceived: neither fornicators, nor idolaters, nor adulterers, nor effeminate, nor abusers of themselves with mankind,

**Leviticus 18:22**= Thou shall not lie with mankind, as with womankind: it is abomination.

**Romans 1:27**= And likewise also the men, leaving the natural use of the woman, burned in their lust one toward another; men with men working that which is unseemly, and receiving in themselves that recompense of their error which was meet.

**Leviticus 19:2**= Speak unto all the congregation of the children of Israel, and say unto them, Ye shall be holy: for I the Lord your God am holy.

**1 Peter 1:16**= Because it is written, Be ye holy; for I am holy.

**Leviticus 19:13**= Thou shall not defraud thy neighbor, neither rob him: the wages of him that is hired shall not abide with thee all night until the morning.

**James 5:4**= Behold, the hire of the laborers who have reaped down your fields, which is of you kept back by fraud, cried: and the cries of them which have reaped are entered into the ears of the Lord of Sabaoth.

**Leviticus 19:15**= Ye shall do no unrighteousness in judgment: thou shall not respect the person of the poor, nor honor the person of the mighty: but in righteousness shall thou judge thy neighbor.

**James 2:1-4**= My brethren, have not the faith of our Lord Jesus Christ, the Lord of glory, with respect of persons. For if there come unto your assembly a man with a gold ring, in goodly apparel, and there come in also a poor man in vile raiment; And ye have respect to him that wear the gay clothing, and say unto him,

Sit thou here in a good place; and say to the poor, Stand thou there, or sit here under my footstool: Are ye not then partial in yourselves, and are become judges of evil thoughts?

**Leviticus 19:17**= Thou shall not hate thy brother in thine heart: thou shall in any wise rebuke thy neighbor, and not suffer sin upon him.

**Matthew 18:15-17**= Moreover if thy brother shall trespass against thee, go and tell him his fault between thee and him alone: if he shall hear thee, thou hast gained thy brother. *But if he will not hear thee, then take with thee one or two more, that in the mouth of two or three witnesses every word may be established. And if he shall neglect to hear them, tell it unto the church: but if he neglects to hear the church, let him be unto thee as a heathen man and a publican.

**1 John 2:9, 11**= He that said he is in the light, and hated his brother, is in darkness even until now. But he that hated his brother is in darkness, and walk in darkness, and know not whither he go, because that darkness hath blinded his eyes.

**1 John 3:15**= Whosoever hated his brother is a murderer: and ye know that no murderer hath eternal life abiding in him.

**Leviticus 19:18**= Thou shall not avenge, nor bear any grudge against the children of thy people, but thou shall love thy neighbor as thyself: I am the Lord.

**Romans 12:19**= Dearly beloved, avenge not yourselves, but rather give place unto wrath: for it is written, Vengeance is mine; I will repay, said the Lord.

**Hebrews 10:30=** For we know him that hath said, Vengeance belongs unto me, I will recompense, said the Lord. And again, The Lord shall judge his people.

**Matthew 5:43-44=** Ye have heard that it hath been said, Thou shall love thy neighbor, and hate your enemy. But I say unto you, Love your enemies, bless them that curse you, do good to them that hate you, and pray for them which despitefully use you, and persecute you;

**Matthew 19:19=** Honor thy father and thy mother: and, Thou shall love thy neighbor as thyself.

**Matthew 22:39=** And the second is like unto it, Thou shall love thy neighbor as thyself.

**Mark 12:31=** And the second is like, namely this, Thou shall love thy neighbor as thyself. There is none other commandment greater than these.

**Luke 10:27=** And he is answering said, Thou shall love the Lord thy God with all thy heart, and with all thy soul, and with all thy strength, and with all thy mind; and thy neighbor as thyself.

**Romans 13:9=** For this, Thou shall not commit adultery, Thou shall not kill, Thou shall not steal, Thou shall not bear false witness, Thou shall not covet; and if there be any other commandment, it is briefly comprehended in this saying, namely, Thou shall love thy neighbor as thyself.

**Galatians 5:14=** For all the law is fulfilled in one word, even in this; Thou shall love thy neighbor as thyself.

**Hebrews 2:8=** Thou hast put all things in subjection under his feet. For in that he put all in subjection under him, he left nothing that is not put under him. But now we see not yet all things put under him.

**James 2:8=** If ye fulfill the royal law according to the scripture, Thou shall love thy neighbor as thyself, ye do well:

**Leviticus 19:32=** Thou shall rise up before the hoary head, and honor the face of the old man, and fear thy God: I am the Lord.

**1 Timothy 5:1-2**= Rebuke not an elder, but intreat him as a father; and the younger men as brethren; The elder women as mothers; the younger as sisters, with all purity.

**Leviticus 20:7**= Sanctify yourselves therefore and be ye holy: for I am the Lord your God.

**1 Peter 1:16**= Because it is written, Be ye holy; for I am holy.

**Leviticus 20:9**= For every one that curse his father, or his mother shall be surely put to death: he hath cursed his father or his mother; his blood shall be upon him.

**Matthew 15:4**= For God commanded, saying, Honor thy father and mother: and He that curse father or mother, let him die the death.

**Leviticus 21:22**= He shall eat the bread of his God, both of the most holy, and of the holy.

**1 Corinthians 9:13**= Do ye not know that they which minister about holy things live of the things of the temple? and they which wait at the altar are partakers with the altar?

**Leviticus 22:20**= But whatsoever hath a blemish, that shall ye not offer: for it shall not be acceptable for you.

**Hebrews 9:14**= How much more shall the blood of Christ, who through the eternal Spirit offered himself without spot to God, purge your conscience from dead works to serve the living God?

**1 Peter 1:19**= But with the precious blood of Christ, as of a lamb without blemish and without spot:

**Leviticus 23:33-34**= And the Lord spoke unto Moses, saying, Speak unto the children of Israel, saying, The fifteenth day of this seventh month shall be the feast of tabernacles for seven days unto the Lord.

**John 7:2**= Now the Jews' feast of tabernacles was at hand.

**Leviticus 24:5**= And thou shall take fine flour and bake twelve cakes thereof: two tenth deals shall be in one cake.

**Hebrews 9:2**= For there was a tabernacle made; the first, wherein was the candlestick, and the table, and the showbread; which is called the sanctuary.

**Leviticus 24:9**= And it shall be Aaron's and his sons'; and they shall eat it in the holy place: for it is most holy unto him of the offerings of the Lord made by fire by a perpetual statute.

**Matthew 12:4**= How he entered into the house of God, and did eat the showbread, which was not lawful for him to eat, neither for them which were with him, but only for the priests?

**Leviticus 24:20**= Breach for breach, eye for eye, tooth for tooth: as he hath caused a blemish in a man, so shall it be done to him again.

**Matthew 5:38**= Ye have heard that it hath been said, An eye for an eye, and a tooth for a tooth:

**Leviticus 25:10**= And ye shall hallow the fiftieth year and proclaim liberty throughout all the land unto all the inhabitants thereof: it shall be a jubilee unto you; and ye shall return every man unto his possession, and ye shall return every man unto his family.

**Luke 4:19**= To preach the acceptable year of the Lord.

**Leviticus 25:43**= Thou shall not rule over him with rigor; but shall fear thy God.

**Colossians 4:1**= Masters, give unto your servants that which is just and equal; knowing that ye also have a Master in heaven.

**Leviticus 26:12**= And I will walk among you, and will be your God, and ye shall be my people.

**2 Corinthians 6:16**= And what agreement hath the temple of God with idols? For ye are the temple of the living God; as God hath said, I will dwell in them, and walk in them; and I will be their God, and they shall be my people.

**Leviticus 26:40**= If they shall confess their iniquity, and the iniquity of their fathers, with their trespass which they trespassed against me, and that also they have walked contrary unto me;

**Luke 15:18**= I will arise and go to my father, and will say unto him, Father, I have sinned against heaven, and before thee,

**1 John 1:9**= If we confess our sins, he is faithful and just to forgive us our sins, and to cleanse us from all unrighteousness.

**Leviticus 26:44**= And yet for all that, when they be in the land of their enemies, I will not cast them away, neither will I abhor them, to destroy them utterly, and to break my covenant with them: for I am the Lord their God.

**Romans 11:2**= God hath not cast away his people which he foreknew. Wot ye not what the scripture saith of Elias? how he makes intercession to God against Israel, saying,

**Leviticus 27:34**= These are the commandments, which the Lord commanded Moses for the children of Israel in mount Sinai.

**Hebrews 12:18-29**= For ye are not come unto the mount that might be touched, and that burned with fire, nor unto blackness, and darkness, and tempest, *And the sound of a trumpet, and the voice of words; which voice they that heard intreated that the word should not be spoken to them any more: (For they could not endure that which was commanded, *And if so much as a beast touch the mountain, it shall be stoned, or thrust through with a dart: *And so terrible was the sight, that Moses said, I exceedingly fear and quake:)

But ye are come unto mount Sion, and unto the city of the living God, the heavenly Jerusalem, and to an innumerable company of angels, To the general assembly and church of the firstborn, which are written in heaven, and to God the Judge of all, and to the spirits of just men made perfect, *And to Jesus the mediator of the new covenant, and to the blood of sprinkling, that speak better things than that of Abel. See that ye refuse not him that speak.

For if they escaped not who refused him that spoke on earth, much more shall not we escape, if we turn away from him that speak from heaven: Whose voice then shook the earth: but now he hath promised, saying, Yet once more I shake not the earth only, but also heaven. And this word,

Yet once more, signified the removing of those things that are shaken, as of things that are made, that those things which cannot be shaken may remain. Wherefore we are receiving a kingdom which cannot be moved, let us have grace, whereby we may serve God acceptably with reverence and godly fear: *For our God is a consuming fire.

*The overwhelming message of Leviticus is the holiness of God "Be holy because I, the Lord your God, is holy." But how can unholy people approach a holy God? The answer first SIN must be dealt with.*

*The opening chapters of Leviticus give detailed instructions for offering sacrifices, which were the active symbols of repentance and obedience. \*Whether bulls, grain, goats, or sheep, the sacrificial offering had to be perfect, with no defects or bruises pictures of the ultimate sacrifice to come, Jesus, the Lamb of God.*

*Jesus has come and opened the way to God by giving up his life as the final sacrifice in our place. \* True worship and oneness with God begin as we confess our sin and accept Jesus Christ as the only one who can redeem us from SIN and HELP us approach GOD. \*Because God the Father, and Jesus Christ the Son Love You, I love you too, we wish for you not to go to Hell, but to Heaven our Heavenly Home, Peace, Love, Joy, Happiness... Light! \*There will be no light in Hell, only Fire, Brimstone torment!*

*What a blessing, hope to see you there In Heaven. \* God the Holy Spirit gave me this idea to write the Bible book this way, for easy reading, and I believe this is true, I hope you be Blessed as I am, I know you will be, read it over, and over again. \*Believe, receive and live a Happy, Healthy, Wealthy, Life in Jesus Christ. \*All things are possible with the Lord God Almighty. \* Love from your Sister in Christ Jesus.*

### Jesus is Lord!

Daily reading: It will bless you. Your spirit is hungry too. Easy reading, for your life, prepare yourself for the life, rest of your life. There is life after death for real. FYI! After death. You should know... this is a reminder book!

*Because we love you!*
*"Jesus is the Way the Truth and the Life"*

*Jesus Christ the Son of the Living God, all almighty, all powerful. All knowing, and all loving. All mighty God all by Himself. Holy, Holy, Holy is the Lord God almighty.*

By: Maryland J. Harrison

*The Word of God!*
*A reminder book to Never forget God,*
*heavenly Father and Lord Jesus Christ,*
*the Son who gave his life for us, all people.*
*Because God loves us, and He want all to be Saved,*
*from the lake of fire. Study the word of God:*
*Abba Heavenly Father.*

*{Psalm 68:11}*

{The Lord gave the word:
great was the company of those that published it}

www.ingramcontent.com/pod-product-compliance
Lightning Source LLC
Chambersburg PA
CBHW060324130626
46553CB00003B/902